PAMELA VANDYKE PRICE
Guide to the wines of Champagne

PITMAN

Associated Companies
Copp Clark Ltd, Toronto
Pitman Publishing New Zealand Ltd, Wellington
Pitman Publishing Pty Ltd, Melbourne

© Pamela Vandyke Price, 1979

First published in Great Britain 1979

All rights reserved. No part of this publication may be reproduced, stored in a retrieval system, or transmitted, in any form or by any means, electronic, mechanical, photocopying, recording and/or otherwise without the prior written permission of the publishers. The paperback edition of this book may not be lent, resold, hired out or otherwise disposed of by way of trade in any form of binding or cover other than that in which it is published, without the prior consent of the publishers. This book is sold subject to the Standard Conditions of Sale of Net Books and may not be resold in the UK below the net price.

Text set in Garamond 10/12
Printed and bound in Great Britain by
Hazell Watson & Viney Ltd, Aylesbury, Bucks
ISBN 0 273 01271 1

Also in this series:

Guide to the Wines of Bordeaux *Pamela Vandyke Price*
Guide to the Wines of Burgundy *Graham Chidgey*
Guide to the Wines of Germany *Hans Siegel*
Guide to the Wines of the Rhône *Peter Hallgarten*
Guide to the Whiskies of Scotland *Derek Cooper*
Guide to the Wines of Spain and Portugal *Jan Read*

This little book on a mighty subject
is affectionately dedicated
to
two friends whose firms represent magnificent Champagnes in the U.K.:
Anthony Leschallas of Mentzendorff
David Rutherford of Rutherford Osborne & Perkin

Their patience in answering many questions
their encouragement in times that have been hard
their enjoyment of several celebrations
owe much to the superb wines they have shared with me
from
Bollinger
and
Roederer
with my love and gratitude

Contents

Acknowledgments — v

1 The Region — 1
Where it is – landscape – climate

2 Champagne's History — 5
The crayères – the early days – an odd 'something' about the wines – Pierre Pérignon – the wine's popularity increases – the Revolution and Napoleon – the British influence – recent history

3 The Vines and the Wines they make — 19
The grapes – how the sparkling wines are made – the still wines – other local drinks

4 The Wine in Bottle — 40
Business arrangements – grandes marques – types of Champagne – the bottle – corks – Champagne labels

5 Visiting the Region — 53
Where to base a stay – when to go – planning a visit – seeing cellars – the Champagne routes

6 Enjoying the Wine — 70
Tasting Champagne – serving Champagne – glasses – Champagne with what? – Champagne drinks

7 Champagne Gastronomy — 95
Meat and fish dishes – sweets and confectionery – cheeses

Acknowledgments

The wine trade are traditionally generous, especially to their students. But so many have contributed to this book by their help to me through the years while I have been trying to learn about Champagne that it would take a long chapter if I were now to cite all those who deserve my thanks. For every Champagne house named, the firms concerned will know that there are many individuals to whom I am indebted; then there are the shippers and merchants in Britain who, representing the Champagne establishments, have obtained information, arranged visits and introductions and been open-handed with bottles. Numerous public relations firms and their staffs have taken much trouble to check material, make inquiries of principals abroad and find pictures, maps and illustrations.

Some friends, however, must be especially thanked. For a long time, the C.I.V.C. have been my kind hosts, as well as being a source of information and guidance on many aspects of Champagne: Monsieur Joseph Dargent and Colonel Bonal have been unsparing in their benevolent concern throughout the preparation of this book and all who use it will owe much to them. In London, the staff of Kingsway Public Relations, notably Malcolm Macintyre and Pat Sherren, have been most patient and efficient colleagues. In particular, I must express my gratitude to Colonel Maurice Buckmaster, for many years a distinguished ambassador of Champagne in Britain who, I am proud to state, obtained for me specialised information needed for the completion of certain chapters.

Other friends who have helped so much begin with John Clevely, M.W., who first taught me about Champagne. With his colleagues past and present at H. Parrot, who represent Veuve Clicquot in the United Kingdom, he has continued the good work. My first study session in Champagne was as a guest of Moët et Chandon, where I was lucky enough to meet Patrick Forbes, at that time compiling his great book; no one can write about Champagne without drawing considerably on this outstanding work. Patrick, his colleagues in London and Épernay, including all those who have welcomed me at the Château de Saran, can never be adequately thanked for all their help and hospitality.

Also during the early days of my visits to Champagne, Tony and Ben Reuss, then representing Pol Roger in Britain, not only gave me much information but introduced me to my dear friends, Monsieur and Madame Christian de Billy and the enchanting Odette Pol Roger. Anthony Leschallas and his colleagues at Mentzendorff gave me the privilege of meeting the late Madame Lily Bollinger, and of enjoying the friendship of the wise and charming Monsieur and Madame Christian Bizot; my friend Cyril Ray's excellent book about Bollinger fails only in one respect – even he is unable to do justice to them in print and I certainly cannot attempt to do so. Their help in many ways has been inestimable.

Among the numerous firms who have shown me much kindness and hospitality in France and, through their representatives, in Britain, I should particularly like to name Ayala, Mercier, Perrier-Jouët, Mumm, Irroy, Castellane and Taittinger. Laurent Perrier have provided much information about Coteaux Champenois and, in London, Frank Arnold has been painstaking about keeping me up to date with this material. To many members of the house of Krug and to David Russell in London I am indebted for many technical details relating especially to this great establishment.

Through French Regional Wines in London I was fortunate enough to meet Jean-Paul Brice and Alain Collery, who enabled me to learn something of the single growth Champagnes as well as a great deal about the region in general. Luc Trouillard enlightened me about a number of aspects of the B.O.B. trade, as well as showing me many of the excellent wines of De Venoge.

The establishment of Abel Lepitre and their United Kingdom representatives handling Champagne de St. Marceaux and George Goulet have been kind enough to advise me about many matters concerning the Champagne world at the present time; their knowledge and clear-sightedness are only surpassed by their kindliness and good humour.

Among the many friends in the British wine trade who have given unsparing help I must especially thank John Lipitch, of R & C Vintners; he has, over the years, helped me understand the various ways in which wines are made sparkling and, by introducing me to the establishment of Pommery & Greno, enabled me to discover many of the historical aspects of Champagne in general and their fine wines in particular. The late Joe Woolley, also C.M. Stevens, M.W., made me aware of the admirable wines of Deutz & Geldermann, and my friends at Laytons introduced me to the very fine wines of Canard Duchêne. David Peppercorn, M.W., first showed me the Saint-Simon wines, and through Taylor Fanshawe I was able to visit the Brun de Neuville co-operative and have the benefit of the advice of Monsieur Mirand. No one, it should be stressed, has ever tried to promote their wines to me – wisely, the great Champagnes have been allowed to speak for themselves.

Years ago I was invited to give the lecture on Champagne and sparkling wines at the now defunct Academy of Wine at Hedges & Butler, and John Davies, M.W., gave me a a great deal of help then. James Long, of Gilbey Vintners has also contributed substantially to my knowledge of the subject, and David Rutherford of Rutherford Osborne & Perkin has been unstinting in his kindness, which included opening for me the firm's last bottle of 1964 Roederer Cristal.

Finally I recall with great affection the late Ronald Avery, who showed me 'pure Avize' and his son, John Avery, M.W., who has introduced me to many fine Champagnes and sparkling wines. Helen Thomson, of O.W. Loeb, has been an especially valued colleague in the work she has done on the manuscript of this book and for much assistance on a visit we made to Champagne.

Pamela Vandyke Price
August – November, 1978

Appendixes

1 Sparkling Wines that are not Champagne — 102

2 The Champagne Wine Fraternity — 105

3 Champagne Festivals — 106

4 Champagne and the Launching of Ships — 107

Glossary — 109

Further Reading — 116

Index — 118

NOTE:
In this book the use of 'Reims' rather than the English version 'Rheims' has been adopted because travellers will see the former on signposts – and on wine labels. In pronouncing names it should be noted that the use of the diaeresis – the two dots over a letter – means that the letter is separately sounded instead of being elided. In certain Champagne names it also involves the sounding of the following consonant, thus Moët is pronounced 'Mo-ette', with the stress on the two syllables, and de Voguë as 'de Vohgooeh'. The last word of the name Perrier-Jouët is pronounced 'Dshoo-ette' – the initial 'J' cannot be exactly reproduced in English. The only other names that I will attempt to indicate are: Bollinger – 'Bollinjay'; Ay – 'Eye' or 'Ay-ee'; Billy – 'Bee-ee'; Heidsieck – 'Hideseek'; Petit Meslier – 'Petty Maylyeh'; Taittinger – 'Tattanjay' and Troyes – 'Trwah'.

P.V.P.

The Region

'La Champagne' is the region, 'le Champagne' the wine and 'la Champagne viticole' is the overall vineyard. The name comes from the Latin *campagna**, signifying open, unforested land. The Champagne vineyards account for something approximating to a hundredth part of all the French regions planted with vines, and there are now about 45,000 acres under vines in the Champagne region. The largest area by far of this overall vineyard is in the Marne; after the Marne Valley comes the Montagne de Reims and then the Côte des Blancs.

Where it is

Champagne is the most northern vineyard in France. It is very extensive, and in former times was a huge province. The *départements* that make up the Champagne area today are those of the Ardennes, Marne, Haute-Marne and Aube. Parts of Champagne, in the north and a strip that curves from the Franco-Belgian frontier almost down to Burgundy, are extremely fertile, although inclined to be flat; this is known as *la Champagne humide* (damp) and includes the region of the Ardennes – wonderful market-garden country and farmland. Adjoining this strip, on the western side, is another which is chalky and very poor; this is known as *la Champagne pouilleuse* (a rude term, signifying 'lousy', 'good for nothing') which, until after World War II, yielded little in the way of crops or grazing lands. Thanks, however, to modern

---

* The word *Champagne* is also used in the Cognac region, where it differentiates those districts which are unforested (Grande and Petite Champagne areas) from those which are wooded (Bois districts).

methods of cultivation and fertilisers, it is now a huge and valuable wheat field.

The Champagne *viticole* area lies within these two strips. It, too, is a chalky land, undulating but not sharply contoured. The Champagne cliffs, or *falaises* as they are sometimes termed, provide admirable sites for the cultivation of vines. The openness of the countryside enables the vineyards to enjoy maximum exposure to sun. The slopes not only keep the vines sufficiently aloof from the dampness and cold of the valleys, they also provide shelter from extremes of wind and rain and facilitate drainage – the vine may like 'to see the river' as it is often said, but it does not thrive if its feet get too wet.

The topsoil here is friable and light in colour, while the subsoil is chalky. It is part of a gigantic layer of chalk that still retains traces of various fossils, sea creatures and certain minerals that are often found in districts associated with elegant, fine wine. Indeed, it is this chalk blanket that, encircling the *falaises* or cliffs that rise above it, spreads out like a wave below the Champagne vineyard and beyond, under the Channel, to reappear as the white cliffs of Dover and the Isle of Wight – and makes it possible to grow vines producing good white wines in many parts of southern England. It is no surprise to English wine makers that the Chardonnay, one of the great Champagne grapes, can flourish on this side of the English Channel too!

If, in walking about in a Champagne vineyard, you can find a place where the earth has been excavated, it is possible to see, in section, the thin, almost powdery topsoil above the whiteness of the chalk subsoil. As the taproot of a vine descends twelve or more feet below ground, the influence of this subsoil is great. The source of water, from which the taproot draws the vine's nourishment, is also greatly affected by the subsoil through which it flows.

Landscape

Champagne as a region is not obviously beautiful or even impressive. The main roads, many of them of Roman origin, cross it like rulers. The villages are plain – clusters of stone houses with a few impressive churches; sometimes, usually hidden in woods or by a river, there will be an elegant château. Superficially, it is an area to cross, in order to get somewhere else. This is what many tourists do. It is what armies, bands of pilgrims, groups of scholars and parties of the nobility have been doing for centuries. Even if you go through a town at what might be expected to be a lively time of day, there are seldom many people about for, apart from around Reims, there is little industry. It appears to be a quiet landscape – until the traveller's attention is caught by a war memorial in a tiny village, burdened with many names; or a trim, carefully-tended military cemetery with headstones extending in an appalling perspective; or when a casual reference in a guidebook mentions the 1917 Champagne vintage being picked by women, children and old men under fire during the Second Battle of the Marne in World War I.

Climate

The climate, while not being particularly attractive, is not usually very cold, but can be wet. Sunshine alone does not make fine wine, but a certain amount of dry warmth is required for the grapes to ripen. Frosts in late spring, especially during the period of the 'Ice Saints' (Pancratius, Servatius, Bonifacio and Sophia) in mid-May, are critical as regards the satisfactory flowering of the vine and setting of the blossom. Wet weather prior to the vintage, causing the grapes to rot or yield to various vine diseases, is another particular hazard.

There are, however, several notable advantages that the Champagne vineyard possesses: the light-coloured soil reflects heat upwards onto the grapes; the undulating slopes enable the air to circulate and keep the vines both warm and dry – a protection against frost; and the region's humidity means that, if the grapes can start to ripen, they will then usually plump out satisfactorily, without risk of being shrivelled by too hot a sun at vintage time. But this very humidity can cause numerous diseases and attacks by pests, which even the most up-to-date pesticides cannot entirely remedy. Worst of all, there is nothing that can be done against a sudden hailstorm. No one who has not seen the effect of even a few moments of hail – which may only affect the vines within an allotment-sized area – can imagine the damage: leaves torn, grapes slit and battered into uselessness or, perhaps early in the season, the stems of the vines bruised so that they look as if someone has been round with a cat-o-nine-tails. Even if the grapes form fairly well after such an assault, the subsequent wine will bear traces of hail and will be somehow skimped, shrill, stalky and mean in character.

It is important to remember these hazards if you are fortunate enough to view an expanse of the Champagne vineyard opulent under the sun, either freshly green in spring or during the wonderful misty days of autumn after the grapes have been picked and when the vine leaves shimmer into bronze, yellow and tawny-crimson before they fall. This is a vineyard where fine wine is made because it is on the very border of where fine wine vines can be cultivated, and it is always at such limits that the vines will yield of their best – but where they are also at greatest risk.

Champagne's History

The history of both the Champagne region and its wine have been well documented for English-speaking readers*, so those who wish can learn the details – which are fascinating as a social and technological account of the influence of the world's greatest sparkling wine. In these pages, however, it is only possible to outline the background of the foil-crowned bottle.

The Crayères

There are numerous huge galleries or *crayères* hollowed out of the chalky underblanket below the vineyard, and many are correctly attributed to the Romans. Sometimes people who have not seen them assume that all the galleries in which the vast stocks of Champagne are stored are *crayères*. This is not so, and the *crayères* are only part of the vast underground network of cellars.

A *crayère* was a Roman excavation, the opening being only about the size of a small ornamental pond – say up to ten feet in diameter and often less. Once the initial hole had been dug, however, the 'chimney' to the surface was progressively extended in size, the area opening out like a huge cone. The chalk, once dug, would have been hauled to the surface and through the comparatively small aperture. Nobody seems quite sure why the Romans worked in this way, but they dug enormous numbers of *crayères* which, subsequently, were often joined together under the earth. It is curious to look up from

---

* Notably in various books by André L. Simon (1877–1970), who started in the wine trade by representing Pommery & Greno in the U.K., and by Patrick Forbes in his magnificent book *Champagne, the Wine, the Land and the People* (Gollancz, 1967).

the bottom of what looks like a cavern, the equivalent of eight or ten storeys below ground, and see a small circle of light above.

It seems impossible that these huge excavations could have been made by men working in semi-darkness with what to us would be very simple tools, yet there are literally hundreds of these hollowed-out cones – Pommery & Greno, for example, have 120 in their cellars; Ruinart, today the oldest Champagne establishment still in production, also have *crayères* that are beautiful in a primitive way as well as impressive. In several establishments the *crayères* have been decorated with sculptures in relief, and Pommery have placed a Virgin and Child in one.

It is arguable, however, whether the Romans used *crayères* for storing wine; they were ideal cool pantries for perishables, and were well protected for reserves of other foodstuffs and goods too. Had the Romans in fact made wine and stored it in the *crayères* in the B.C. era, it seems likely that Julius Caesar (c. 100–44 B.C.), who was a meticulous reporter, would certainly have mentioned it in his account of his conquest of Gaul. True, Pliny the Elder (A.D. 23–79) is said to

Champagne bottles in a Roman crayère

have referred to the wines of Reims in general and Ay in particular as "for the king's table", but Mr Forbes has gone through the extant works of this writer and cannot find the statement.

The finding of a fossil of a vine near Sézanne, which can be dated as belonging to the remote prehistoric period, is thought by some to indicate that vines were cultivated in this area from that time. But *Vitis sezannensis* is nowadays thought to be a type of wild grape which, even if it had been edible, was unlikely to have been used for wine-making on account of the sharp, sour type of wine which it would have produced if used for a fermented beverage.

The Early Days

Evidence indicates that the Champagne vineyards were probably established in the first century A.D. From this time wines were produced, in spite of all sorts of man-made difficulties: imperial edicts from Emperor Domitian in A.D. 92 ordering the uprooting of the vines – though I have always wondered how thoroughly the wily peasants obeyed this (these edicts were repealed by Emperor Probus in A.D. 280); a succession of invasions across the open defenceless plain, including the devastations of Attila the Hun in the fifth century; and years when the weather was so bad that the wine makers, possessing only primitive knowledge, must have found it was simply impossible to produce wine at all.

In 496 Clovis, King of the Franks, was baptised, together with a large number of his army, by Saint Rémi, Bishop of Reims. For years I thought that Reims got its name from Rémi, but it appears that it derives from the Remi tribe of early Gaul, when it was a very large settlement and the chief city of that region of northern France. 'Rheims' is, in fact, the original spelling of the name, which was only changed in French in the late eighteenth century; some romantic Rémois still believe that Reims was founded by Remus, brother of the Romulus who founded Rome.

From the time of Clovis' baptism Reims became very important as the place where all the kings of France were crowned. Even if they had actually had a crown put on their heads elsewhere, in some emergency, it was to Reims they came to be anointed, like Clovis. At his coronation the crowd became so dense that Rémi could not be handed the consecrated oil, so the Bishop uttered a prayer, in reply to which a dove descended carrying an ampulla of holy oil. "Kings of France are made at Reims," said Joan of Arc to the future Charles VII. Naturally the Rémois enjoyed many material advantages from the tradition of coronations and the increasing importance of the great cathedral, which is an outstanding Gothic masterpiece.

Possibly the constant threat of wars and invasions inculcated a piety into the Champenois temperament. Patrick Forbes states that Épernay, which Clovis gave to Saint Rémi – who owned many vineyards – has been "burnt, pillaged or sacked on twenty-five occasions." The great underground galleries were used as refuges through the centuries. During the early medieval period, when the great religious establishments were the strongholds of learning, research and art, as well as of piety, many orders of monks and nuns flourished in Champagne. They ran schools, hospices for travellers, nursing-homes and dispensaries, providing a chain of places to stay in conjunction with their brother and sister houses throughout western Europe. There was much coming and going between the religious themselves, and the houses were visited by travellers of all kinds, from pilgrims and scholars to merchants and the nobility. The interchange of information and knowledge kept the residents in touch with the great events of the world and enabled them to influence many social as well as political matters.

Wine was, of course, required for sacramental use. But it is often not realised that, at this time, it had many other uses: as a disinfectant should the water supply be questionable, for washing wounds, as a stimulant for the convalescent, a sedative for the sick, and as a marinade, so that foods could be tenderised and rendered fairly safe to eat. Even when wines became soured and turned into vinegar, there were still many cleansing and disinfecting properties they possessed for human beings and their animals, as well as in the kitchen. It would have been unusual for anyone, except the very poor, to travel without some form of wine and, in a producing region, wine was daily utilised in numerous ways.

The Champenois religious houses were frequently endowed with vineyards as legacies from pious families. The religious orders enjoyed a type of priority, together with the nobility, in being allowed to put their wines on the market before the ordinary growers and, because of the efficiency and low running costs of the monastic holdings, the wines they produced were both cheaper and, usually, better than the others. Pope Urban II, in the eleventh century, said that the wines of Ay were supreme – but he was a Champagne man by birth.

The wines of Champagne began to be noticed outside the region as early as 1200, and they were mentioned in the poem "The Battle of the Wines" which appraised different ones. It is a tribute to the stubborn determination of wine growers that, even through the Hundred Years' War, in the fourteenth and fifteenth centuries, the Champenois continued to receive compliments on their produce.

Emperors made huge detours so as to drink Ay on its home ground, and on at least one occasion got too drunk to keep a rendezvous with the King of France. Edward III of England, besieging Reims in 1359, captured many casks of wine and, in 1417, the Duke of Burgundy decided he would take over Champagne – an intention bitterly opposed by the constantly invading English who, even when Joan of Arc drove them out and Charles VII was crowned at Reims, went off with huge stocks of wine, while the wretched Champenois huddled in their cellars. Even when peace was – at least vaguely – restored, the religious wars made the production of fine wine fearfully difficult. But it continued to be made. Indeed, in the sixteenth century François I of France, the Emperor Charles V, Henry VIII of England and Pope Leo X all had dealings with Ay vineyards: they kept agents there and even had their own wineries to make sure of the quality of the wine they bought. Henri IV, known as "*le vert galant*", once snubbed a pompous Spanish ambassador, who was intoning his master's numerous titles, by referring to himself as simply the "Lord of Ay". And today, if one remarks with surprise on the quality of an Ay Champagne, the rebuke will be definite – "It was the wines of Ay that made the reputation of Champagne."

An odd 'Something' about the Wines

Some accounts of Champagne state that up to this time the wines were red, but this term seems capable of a variety of interpretations and was probably used to indicate a range from light tawny to pink – not a true red. The coolness of the Champagne vineyard means that the pigments in the skins of the black grapes seldom develop enough to colour the wine to what we understand by the term 'red'; *vin gris* or 'grey wine' was often all that might be achieved – in other words, pale rosé.

However, there was always an odd 'something' about the Champagne wines; the spring after they had been made they tended to develop a fizzy style – well, this was simply part of the process of fermentation, the wine beginning to 'work' again when the warmth of the new season stimulated the action of the yeasts to a minor turbulence in the wine. This, as with other wines, would eventually cease by early summer. However, Champagne wines seemed to have more of this 'liveliness' than was usual. Sometimes they bubbled in a truly mad fury, although at others they were apparently quite still, possibly just seeming to 'prickle' slightly in the mouth. This vivacity was pleasing to many consumers, but it appeared to be present without any special reason and, as wines were still moved and kept in wooden casks, this liveliness passed as the wine became old. This was due to constant exposure to the air through the porous wood and also within the cask, because the amount of air inside increased as the wine was drawn off.

Then, in the seventeenth century, several sets of circumstances resulted in a major alteration in the production of the wines of Champagne. At this time the English glassworks began to make bottles that were so good that they were in great demand, not only in England but also in export markets – notably the wine regions. Up to Elizabethan times such glass bottles as did exist were used only as carafes or as a means of moving liquids from cellar to table, but not for storing wine. Corks, too, were known in England as excellent stoppers, tied on to the bottles with packthread; the bark of the cork oak, which flourishes in the Iberian Peninsula, had been used to stopper amphorae even in Roman times, but knowledge of it had been mainly lost. It is not certain how the bark came to England and became used for sealing bottles (of ale as well as wine) but, with the trading between Portugal and England and contacts with Spain – the English were not always fighting the Spaniards – the use of cork was established, even though it remained unknown in France for some time to come.

At the coronation at Reims of Louis XIV, a group of rich young nobles, most of them with estates in Champagne, began to make themselves known as great gourmets and, more importantly, as publicists for Champagne. These gentry were the founders of the Ordre des Coteaux (see page 105) and, at the magnificent and extravagant court of the Sun King, their wines achieved enormous chic. When one of them, the Marquis de Saint-Evremond, somehow offended the pompous King and was exiled in England, he arranged for his favourite drink – mostly the wine of his friend the Marquis de Sillery – to be sent over in cask and bottled in London. The wine delighted the exuberant court of the newly restored Charles II, "the Merry Monarch". Champagne was praised in numerous plays and verses and quaffed in quantity by the men and women of London's smart set. The British began their long love affair with the lively wine.

Pierre Pérignon

Yet these events merely prepared the way for the master-work of a Benedictine monk who, in the late 1660s, became cellarmaster at the already important Abbey of Hautvillers. This establishment, which then possessed greatly revered relics of Saint Helena, mother of Constantine the Great and discoverer of the True Cross, had been founded in the seventh century as the result of a miraculous vision and it was a great place of pilgrimage, as well as a centre of learning. Benedictines travelled between the different houses of their order, and there are several theories as to how the use of cork was brought to them in Champagne. Some theories assert that the young Benedictine Pierre Pérignon might have worked for a time in one of the Spanish or Catalan monasteries and there seen the utilisation of cork as a stopper; certainly, in the south-east of France, the wine makers of Limoux had begun to make what is now registered as *Le plus vieux brut du monde* – a sparkling wine, with the sparkle retained in the bottle by a firmly-held cork. Or it may have been that monks coming up from Spain en route for one of the Benedictine establishments in Germany brought cork-stoppered vessels as part of their travelling equipment, and the Hautvillers monks showed these to their cellarmaster.

Pierre Pérignon was certainly a remarkable man. It is said that, even when he had gone blind in old age, he could detect, by smelling, the origin of the grapes brought to him from different plots of vineyards. It is for his masterly composition of the *cuvée*, or base wine, that he is most respected by producers. Instead of simply making the wine cask by cask, according to whichever lot of grapes was being picked, he would combine the various pickings of the grapes so that the fruitiness of one small plot might be freshened by the crisp acidity of the wine from another; or the full, perfumed style coming from one vineyard would be balanced by the delicacy of that from another patch of soil.

He seems also to have been the first person to have made a wholly successful and definitely red still wine, and to have appreciated the contribution that could be made by black grapes to the sparkling wine that was so vastly improved by his skill. Soon buyers, even from outside Champagne, were asking specifically for 'Pérignon wines'.

The Wine's Popularity Increases

Thus the suitable bottle, the efficient closure and the growing publicity for the wines of Champagne contributed to the wonderful achievement of a great wine maker – and, during the next few decades, the sparkle was established in Champagne and the wine's popularity increased. The courts of England and France revelled in the bubbly wine, although the English continued to drink vast amounts of the still Champagne as well, both red and white. The great London clubs, many of them founded in the eighteenth century, cellared huge quantities of Champagne. It was served at pleasure gardens such as London's Vauxhall, to those taking the waters at Bath, and it appears to have been the unquestioned choice of refreshment for 'little suppers', whether for a party or a twosome, throughout fashionable European capitals. Madame de Pompadour's praise: "It is the only wine that leaves a woman beautiful after drinking," was an invaluable recommendation.

Although enormous amounts of still wine continued to be made, the late eighteenth and early nineteenth centuries saw the rise of many of the great Champagne houses known today: Clicquot-Ponsardin, Lanson, Ruinart, the three Heidsiecks, Moët et Chandon, and others. Methods of production were improved, science ensured that the wine's vivacity could be controlled and its appeal increased, even in countries as distant as Russia and India, as well as in the huge markets of Germany and the United States – although Britain remained the most important export customer.

The Revolution and Napoleon

The *crayères* sheltered many Champenois in the French Revolution, and Madame Clicquot was actually married in a cellar because the churches were deconsecrated. It was at Ste. Ménéhould that the fleeing French Royal Family were recognised and taken back to their deaths in Paris. The horrible Revolutionaries swigged Champagne copiously, and Danton even bathed in it. Napoleon is supposed to have said "Champagne banishes etiquette", but he is hardly to be ranked with discriminating drinkers.

Abroad, such supplies as could be got out of France commanded popularity and high prices: Beau Brummell used Champagne in his special recipe for boot blacking, the Prince Regent ordered supplies of Sillery to be sent to Carlton House Terrace and to Brighton; in Dresden in 1800 Sir William and Lady Hamilton drank enormous quantities with Lord Nelson, Emma astonishing the company by her capacity.

Blücher, leading the Russian, Prussian and Austrian armies into France against Napoleon in 1814, was said to be inspired in his advance by the thought of drinking Champagne on its home ground, and so Reims fell to the Cossacks. It was later retaken by the French, when Napoleon enjoyed the hospitality of both Monsieur Ponsardin, Madame Clicquot's brother, and the Mayor, Jean-Rémy Moët. Later, a huge review was held there to celebrate Napoleon's final defeat and the Tsar of Russia stayed in Vertus, to the extreme embarrassment of the little town where accommodation was very limited. The troops were inspected by the Emperor of Austria, the King of Prussia, the Prince Royal of Bavaria and the Duke of Wellington. The Champenois became heartily sick of these disturbances to their lives, but the Russians took home with them such a liking for Champagne that, until the Revolution of 1917, they were the second most important export market for the wine.

The British Influence

In Victorian England the 'Marlborough House set', intimates of the then Prince of Wales, later Edward VII, made Champagne fashionable. It was popular not only in the restaurant and at the supper table (especially when the 'stage door Johnnies' took out the stars of the musical entertainments and ballet) but also as a refreshment on the race course and at the butts, where a shout of 'Boy!' from one of the guns or his loader would bring somebody running up with bottles. Boys at Eton in the 1860s used to write home for Champagne to serve at supper with friends. The masters approved, as they felt it distinguished the school!

By the late nineteenth century the British preference for a dry wine began to affect all Champagne producers, many of whom mainly made sweetish wines (which their Russian and South American customers liked). The first really dry Champagnes came to Britain in quantity in 1865, but the major change in the style of the wine seems to have taken place during the aftermath of the Franco-Prussian War (1870–71), when once again the Champagne region was occupied by the Germans as part of the payment for the war. However, some houses had to wait until the older, sweet-toothed generation among their directors died out before they could start making a truly dry wine.

When Professor George Saintsbury's *Notes on a Cellar-Book* was published in 1920, the author refers to sweet Champagne as indicating "a period so far back that only the oldest of us remembers it." Saintsbury thought that, at the time when he began his famous – even notorious – record, any wine lists including dry Champagne really referred to "still dry Sillery". He commented that then, "at any rate in the country, Clicquot was more often still sweet – not to the 'Russe' extent, which was only for savages or children, but yet not dry." His book illustrates some of the attitudes of would-be connoisseurs of his day, and his report of the comment of his 'Pall Mall mentor' (the sort of wine merchant I should probably have described as a "precious snob") is interesting. When Saintsbury told this man that he did not share "the prevailing mania for Pommery", the merchant looked at him approvingly and said "I'd nearly as soon have a bra-a-andy and sod-d-a!" (implying distaste for dry Champagnes).

The 'dry' Pommerys of the 1890s (the Prince of Wales' favourite was 1892 Pommery) would not, I think, have been shrilly dry, if the style of the present day can be associated in any way with the wines that were made eighty years ago. The house of Pommery makes what to me is a gracious wine, with plenty of fruit and marked maturity. But if you think of this type of Champagne in relation to the sort of drinker who had been accustomed to very full, almost fat, wines which demonstrate the 'Pinot Noir' style, then you will appreciate that the 'dry' Pommery would have struck the palate of the 'mentor' so that he would certainly have noticed it; I would not, myself, have accepted a brandy and soda as an alternative to a wine that I happened to find too dry – but the man sounds unreceptive to anything new, however good. It is significant that those who scorned the dry Champagnes lost as much enjoyment as those who, today, scorn the sweet ones. The lover of wine should keep an open mind.

As always, prophecies of doom attended every major change; the late André Simon thought that modern techniques detracted from the individual styles of the houses' wines and regretted that the 1893s were the last Champagnes to possess distinctive personality, house by house. Yet in 1978 I saw a young trainee wine merchant identify six non-vintages out of eight in a blind tasting! Each house definitely still possesses its individual character.

Champagne was very much a 'Belle Époque' wine, celebrated in such music-hall numbers as *Champagne Charlie* and the Champagne polka, as well as in Johann Strauss's acclamation of Champagne in *Die Fledermaus*. No one, however, seems to have evidence of its use in the bath at this time, although one elderly writer between the wars thought that, as a boy, he remembered seeing on sale in Paris a Champagne '*pour le bain*'.

The British were drinking more and more. The young men about town in the novels of Thackeray and Trollope are credited with drinking Champagne almost exclusively. A British gastronomic writer of the late Victorian period does affirm that, in Paris, Champagne was not drunk at dinner "but in London the climate and the taste of the fair sex go before orthodox rules". Wine merchant Frank Hedges Butler, a pioneer of early motoring and ballooning, would ascend to the heavens using his firm's Champagne (Delmotte) as ballast, flinging out the empties when he wanted to go higher. His chauffeur, following his route in a horseless carriage, would appease and pay the owners of shattered conservatories and greenhouses, giving them a price list of the firm at the same time.

However, life in the Edwardian era, in the sense of entertaining and taking a drink, was becoming less formal, so that Champagnes made solely for serving with or after food tended to give some place to wines that could be enjoyed more casually, between times, with 'suppers' or other simple refreshment. Remember that at the turn of the century the apéritif was unknown (meals were served on time and no alcohol was needed as a social ice-breaker) and, in Britain, oysters were never served at formal meals (they might be considered as the Edwardian equivalent of today's baked beans). However, the custom of 'Champagne and a chicken' as a way of reconciling lovers, which had originated much earlier, was still relevant and was the cause of much Edwardian tippling of Champagne.

Recent History

The vine pest, *phylloxera vastatrix*, struck Champagne somewhat later than other French vineyards, so that the wine could continue to be made even while other areas were unable to produce; replanting of resistant American stock onto which the requisite vines could then be grafted began at the turn of the century, but was not really completed until after World War I.

In the early part of the twentieth century, the 'Champagne riots' disturbed the region. Up to this time, not only was the Champagne-producing area much larger than it is today, but also grapes grown quite outside the region were allowed to be sold to makers of Champagne, especially if the local harvest was poor or scarce; even southern wines, of poor quality, might be brought in and made sparkling. French Government legislation, in attempting to protect Champagne, laid down exactly where grapes for Champagne could be grown – thereby infuriating the wine makers of the Aube who, reasonably enough, considered themselves as forming part of the overall Champagne vineyard, but who were left out of the demarcated region. Dissatisfaction turned into anger after the bad vintage in 1909.

In 1910 the *vignerons* (wine makers) became violent and, armed with uprooted vine props and vineyard tools, broke into many premises to destroy supplies of suspect wine. Literal rivers of Champagne flowed through many streets. Troops went into action in Épernay and Hautvillers in 1911 and, in Ay, women threw themselves in front of the cavalry to prevent charges; the house of Geldermann and forty-one other buildings and warehouses were set on fire and destroyed, six establishments at Damery and others at Dizy suffering the same fate. The mob, by now hardly knowing what they were doing, also set fire to the wholly impeccable firms of Ayala and Bissinger at Ay – these firms, confident of their security because no wine from outside Champagne had ever been received by them, had not set any guard. Bollinger escaped – the rioters actually lowered their red flag as they went marching past that house – but the effects of the violence were appalling in the rest of the tiny town. The military remained in the area until vintage time; fortunately conditions were good, the vintagers went out to pick and the soldiers could leave. Subsequent laws established exactly what Champagne and the region were, and also defined *vin mousseux* and *vin gazéifié* in terms that still stand today.

In September 1914 the Germans once again occupied Reims. The First Battle of the Marne took place but, in spite of the shortage of vintagers, the 1914 vintage was a fine one. Maurice Pol Roger, then Mayor of Épernay, was one of the heroes of the period; he assisted such pickers as could get to the vineyards and, eventually, issued notes of currency against his own name. He was so respected that, when the Germans tried to disrupt the economy at the end of the war, his courage enabled business to continue. Later, when peace was restored, Maurice Pol Roger fought a duel with the *Préfet* of the Marne who, he considered, was guilty of cowardice and desertion of his post at the time of crisis. During the war Reims was terribly damaged in 1,051 days of bombardment. Pictures of the time show huge piles of ruins and widespread destruction. People lived in the cellars and, by 1918, the damage was so great that the remaining civilians were ordered to leave. The Allied soldiers, with hope almost gone, were able to save the city – it is said they were inspired by the thought that "As long as there is Champagne in Reims, we'll defend it!"

It is astonishing, considering where the terrible fighting took place (much of it on the northern slopes of the Montagne de Reims) that the vines could then be tended at all. Many people were killed in the vineyards, including at least 20 children, while picking the 1914 vintage. The war graves record the deaths of French, British, American, Italian, Moroccan and even Russian combatants in many parts of the Champagne region. It is a wonder that wine could still be made, much less a wine involving such skill as Champagne; yet, even under fire, the vines were tended, the grapes picked and, in the cellars, women took over from men the detailed after-care of the wine.

Between the two world wars Champagne continued to be the delight of wine lovers, in spite of Prohibition in the U.S., economic depression in many parts of Europe – and the competition of other, cheaper sparkling wines that began to be made in many regions of France and in other countries. Some of the most dreary years of this period – 1920, 1921, 1928 and 1929 – were excellent Champagne vintages. Yet the area, as it was then and is now, represents only about half that of the Champagne vineyards in 1818. In 1927 the Champagne vineyard was defined; it extends over 75,000 acres, all of which were under vines in the nineteenth century, but now only 45,000 acres are actually devoted to vine growing.

World War II was in some ways even more terrible for the Champenois than its predecessor – this time, as well as the sinister circumstances of the German occupation, there were the shortages of corks, bottles and labour. Stocks were requisitioned for Germany (unless their owners had been able to wall them up and hide them), such orders often being totally unreasonable and impossible to fulfil (although many were also deliberately misrouted).

The Resistance was active in the area and firms that were trying to help them or simply attempting to maintain their work risked heavy fines, imprisonment and deportation. Comte Robert de Vogüé and two colleagues in his firm were arrested and the Comte was condemned to death, but he and a colleague spent the rest of the war in concentration camps; other firms which protested at this action were fined huge sums. The one good thing about this time was the establishment, in 1941, of the Comité Interprofessionnel du Vin de Champagne, usually referred to as the C.I.V.C., which continues its work to the present day.

With peace restored, Champagne sales – including those of the wines that had been hidden during the occupation – soared again. There was a time when Britain slipped from being the biggest customer for the world's supreme sparkler, but whichever of the applications of the maxim "In victory you deserve it, in defeat you need it" is pertinent, at the end of 1978 Britain was second only to Italy as the top export market. It is slightly ominous to reflect that, in economic crises and wars, the consumption of Champagne invariably rises!

Technical improvements in caring for fine wine have made more Champagne available everywhere. Whether the bottle is opened to coax appetite back to an invalid, seal a domestic reconciliation, celebrate a special triumph or anniversary or just create an instant party atmosphere, there is and can be only one wine as the first choice.

The Vines and the Wines they make

There are several grape varieties permitted for cultivation to make Champagne, but certain types which have been found to be outstanding in the way they yield and withstand disease are now the vines most cultivated. The foundations of Champagne are the 'Pinot', which is a black grape, and the 'Chardonnay', which is white. Two other varieties, the 'Petit Meslier' and the 'Arbanne', are allowed to be cultivated by law, but these grapes have practically disappeared nowadays. There are endless sub-varieties of grapes related to the great classics of the world of wine, and literally dozens of 'Pinots' are in existence, but the two grown in Champagne are the Pinot Noir and the Pinot Meunier. Between them, they account for about three-quarters of the vines in the whole Champagne vineyard.

The Pinot is a most interesting and influential vine; it produces the black grape that makes the red Burgundies of the Côte d'Or, certain red table wines of the Douro Valley in Portugal and, as the 'Tinta Francisca' (its name there) it also contributes to port. But, in considering the two main vine varieties of Champagne, it must always be remembered that, although a grape will in some ways retain its basic style, it will also be greatly influenced by being produced in a different climate and on different soil. The 'micro-climates' prevailing in quite small patches of the region, different from those of vineyards even a hundred yards away, mean that even exactly the same grape varieties, grown on what is apparently the same kind of soil, will produce an appreciably individual type of wine. This makes generalisations difficult and unreliable.

People who try to link the still red wines of Champagne to red Burgundies, or the still whites to white Burgundies, are complicating their appraisal. Of course the Pinot, wherever it grows, and the Chardonnay, wherever it is pressed, will make wines that retain certain family characteristics. I have my own tags to these grape varieties as regards the wines they make: the Pinot has a somewhat intense, soft fragrance that is almost a perfume, with a gracious, velvety flavour and a delicate freshness as it leaves the palate. The Chardonnay I find somewhat reserved as to bouquet, but with a lingering fascination that pierces the sense of smell and registers itself with a trail of after-taste; the flavour of a wine made from the Chardonnay is compact, at first often seeming slight – but it builds to an ample stature, and the after-taste is elegantly crisp and fresh. But these are personal *aides-mémoires*; they should not be adopted if you do not share them – and if you can compose your own similes, so much the better.

There are many reasons why a Pinot or Chardonnay is influenced as regards smell, taste, weight and after-taste by its vineyard, the climate, and the way the wine is made. Also, if comparisons with other wines are to be helpful, then it is essential to bear in mind the type of wine that the producer wants to make. Keep the family likeness of the great vine varieties as mere likenesses, not necessarily anything closely akin. In the U.S., for example, a wine can be labelled as "Chardonnay" when there is a mere 51 per cent of this variety contributing to it – but even 10 per cent of something else may make a wine differ radically from one that is 75 per cent or 100 per cent Chardonnay from the same or a different vineyard.

The Grapes

The Pinot is supposed to get its name from the way the smallish black grapes cling tightly together in a pine cone shape (Latin *pinus*). Patrick Forbes instances the frequency of vines resembling the Pinot in Champagne church sculptures (the vine is constantly used as a decoration in church art, both because of Christ's statement "I am the true vine"[*] and because a bunch of grapes was used to signify the church itself). There are numerous varities of Pinot but the Pinot Noir, with its very dark-coloured grapes, which are a blue-violet when ripe, and with leaves that are only slightly serrated, is the most important. These grapes are so covered with bloom at vintage time that they look as if they have been sprayed with sugar. The Pinot Meunier gets its name because of the whitish down on the leaves, which are as if powdered with flour (*meunier* is French for miller). This grape is

[*] *John*, 15, i

intensely dark when fully ripe and is a sturdier vine than the Pinot Noir, therefore it is useful for planting in exposed patches of a vineyard.

The Chardonnay is a grape that is now referred to correctly by its single name and not, as formerly, the Pinot Chardonnay – for it has nothing to do with the Pinot family. It is a somewhat sensitive vine, the rather irregular, loosely composed bunches usually ripening after the black grapes of the region; these 'white' grapes are actually pale celadon green and when fully ripe they can have a slightly golden tinge on their skins. The contribution the Chardonnay makes to Champagne is in providing the zip, finesse and clear-cut, racy 'breed' of a fine wine. It is also the vine that makes *blanc de blancs*.

Blanc de blancs is a term that is, in my opinion, used too much and without intelligence. What it means is, literally, "white from whites" – that is, a white wine made from white grapes. It is correctly used in Champagne to denote a wine that is, indeed, made solely from the white grapes permitted in the region: the result can be a delicious, light-bodied, crisp wine. But the insistence of that popular fictional hero, James Bond, on ordering "Blanc de blancs" gave many people the idea that this must be 'the best' Champagne. It is nothing of the sort. One might say that it is good for apéritif drinking or, as I once somewhat affectedly wrote, "a morning Champagne". As made by certain Champagne establishments, using the wines of certain selected vineyards and *cuvées*, a *blanc de blancs* can be an aristocrat of Champagne, even used to make the luxury version of the house. But it is not inevitably 'the best'. As for other table wines, labelled as "Sauvignon – blanc de blancs", what else could a white wine made from a white grape possibly be? As used in Champage the term is useful and sensible – elsewhere, tautologous and pandering to the public weakness for fancy names.

A *blanc de noirs* is a white wine made solely from black grapes. This is rather a rarity, even in France, and at one time it was usually described as a wine possessing body and fruit but somewhat lacking in finesse. I certainly thought this might be so from the few occasions on which I had tasted this type of wine, but then I was shown some of the single vineyard wines of Ay – when it was impossible to associate products of such delicacy and finesse with anything other than unqualified praise, and wonder that they could have been made solely from black grapes. The Ay vineyard possesses a quality inherent in all the wines it makes, and certain *blancs de noirs* made there are very fine. Other particular styles of Champagne are dealt with on pages 42–46.

How the Sparkling Wines Are Made

From the moment that the vintagers go out to pick the grapes, extreme care is exercised at every stage in the making of the wine. The C.I.V.C. (see page 41), in conjunction with growers, producers and a government representative, establish the price that is to be paid for the grapes coming from the various specific vineyards. (Vineyard in this sense means an overall vineyard and not necessarily one site, plot or 'growth' in the way that this word is used in other wine regions, to indicate an individual estate.)

The vineyards are graded according to the quality of the grapes. Those that are usually excellent and that, in the particular year being considered, promise equal quality, are rated as '100 per cent'. This means that owners of plots in these vineyards can ask the top price permitted for the grapes vintaged there. This term – *'cent pour cent'* – can be confusing, as some people get the impression that it refers to the location where the grapes are grown; of course, it does – but a Champagne made from '100 per cent' vineyards is one that contains only grapes grown in those vineyards approved as deserving to get the full or top price. Other vineyards are graded down to 77 per cent, according to the quality of their grapes.

The Vintage

The vintage in all vineyards throughout the world generally takes place one hundred days after the flowering of the vine in the spring. This naturally varies according to the weather, but in Champagne the vintage can be later than in the rest of France because of the northern location of this vineyard. It may be mid-September, but it can be as late as mid-October or as early as August. Vintagers tend to come from the northern and eastern French towns, many of them from industrial centres, and their ancestors for generations have taken a working holiday in Champagne, recruited by the agents of Champagne establishments in the cities. The work is hard and concentrated, so that students and those who hope to earn holiday money by a little grape picking are likely to have an unpleasant surprise!

The vintage should be completed within ten to fourteen days – this is important if the grapes are not to develop rot or the weather to break – and, in addition to hot sun, there can be rain at this time, which means subsequent mud. Work starts as early in the day as possible because the grapes ought to reach the presshouse cool, so that fermentation does not start in the piles of fruit. Vintagers snip off the bunches of grapes with a pair of scissor-like cutters (*épinettes*), put them into their individual baskets and, when these are full, they are tipped into huge wicker oval containers (*mannequins*), each of which holds 176 lb (80 kg) of fruit. Today these traditional receptacles are often replaced by wooden boxes or plastic containers, which are easier to pack into the lorries for transport to the presshouse.

If there is any doubt as to whether all the grapes picked are in prime condition, then it may be necessary to involve the process known as *épluchage*: the word *éplucher* means to clean, pick over, sort out, review and, in this context, it necessitates sorting the grapes out in the vineyard, picking by picking. *Épluchage* is a highly skilled operation, because those going through the grapes must be experienced in knowing exactly what they are watching out for as regards imperfections, and able in a second to detect even the slightest rot, damage or trace of disease. The process is carried out by these skilled workers as the grapes arrive from the pickers, before they are loaded to go to the press.

A wicker tray, called a *clayette*, is propped between two *mannequins* or baskets, the grapes are spread out on this tray and the *éplucheurs* work through the bunches. It is up to the individual wine maker to decide whether and when *épluchage* shall take place; of course, it adds considerably to the ultimate cost of the wine because it takes time, costs money (to pay the skilled operators), and involves a loss of the crop in the form of the discarded grapes. There are many views about this process. Although it is authoritatively declared that it will always be done on demand, there are many occasions when it is quite unnecessary, but also others when the person making the decision as to whether one part of a vineyard needs the additional care of *épluchage* has to weigh against this the difficulties and expense involved – suppose rain threatens and everyone is hastening to get the vintage in, suppose the possible imperfections are very slight and could be corrected by the skill of the wine maker, suppose the need for an abundant vintage is great? Modern vine cultivation and care protects the grapes against many of the hazards that threatened them in the past, and because present-day costs at every stage of the making of

The process of épluchage

a bottle of Champagne are so inescapably high, the decision to increase these is an extremely difficult one.

In discussing *épluchage* with a number of those whose opinions I respect, I have listened to several views – from the extremes of those who say that the process is rarely carried out today and that technical know-how makes it largely unnecessary, to those who say that they are among the very few firms who still do carry out *épluchage* as part of their vineyard routine (although, of course, not constantly nor in every part of the vineyard). I am sure that all who spoke to me were sincere. The majority probably make use of the process when it is absolutely necessary, but tend to have the picking-over done little bunch by little bunch instead of grape by single grape, which is the traditional method. *Épluchage* is an established part of the making of Champagne, but nowadays you may have to ask around if you are to see it taking place in the vineyards.

The last day of the vintage is traditionally a time for rejoicing and feasting. Many of the old customs have died with time, but a lavish celebration meal (the *Cochelet*)* still takes place after the last flower-garlanded load of grapes has gone to the presshouse, and songs and toasts end the hard work of the vintagers.

The base wine

Champagne can only be made on the foundation of a fine wine with certain characteristics: it must be fairly high in acidity, with definite robustness of character and the capability of developing additional subtleties with maturation. This is why, even with detailed attention to the Champagne process, wines from hot vineyards, which tend to be low in acidity, or of insipid or superficial style and inability to develop with age, simply cannot sustain this method of making them sparkling. Patrick Forbes rightly says that: "with the sole exception of the Champagne district" (but he must be allowed a certain partiality here) "carbonic acid gas has the effect of intensifying a wine's characteristics to that wine's detriment: a poor wine becomes poorer still; the delicate balance of qualities to be found in a perfect wine is upset."

If you want to know how good a Champagne is – or any other wine made by the Champagne method – then pour a helping into a glass; cover it with a piece of paper and leave it overnight or long enough for it to go quite flat. Then taste it – and you will know the quality of the base wine.

Pressing

The traditional Champagne press is called a *maie*. It can be square but it is usually round, made of wood, with a series of paling-like sections forming the sides. A lid comes down onto the top of the grapes to squeeze out the juice – it is important that this is done quickly because, as with any fine white wine, the fermentation must not start before the pressing, and the pigments in the skins of the grapes must not tint the 'must' (unfermented grape juice), which is pale greenish-yellow. The juice that runs from the press is separately stored, according to whether it is the result of the first, second or subsequent squeezings. The contents of each whole *maie* will be about 4,000 kg, and these will yield up to 3,000 litres of must. The quantity depends on the

---

* So-called either because a cockerel (*coq*) was traditionally killed for the occasion or, as some think, because a piglet (*cochon*) was the central part of the festivities.

grape varieties being pressed, because the Chardonnay yields more than the Pinot.

In some parts of the region it is possible to see presses of the type that enable the grapes to be pressed inside a horizontal cylinder by the gradual swelling of a large bag, which gently squeezes the grapes against the cylinder. But these presses, although they will be familiar to visitors of many other wine regions, are infrequently used in Champagne, except by certain co-operatives.

The various pressings are important, because the first pressings yield the finer quality of juice. The first 2,000 litres of juice are the *vin de cuvée* which, kept apart, can make 2,500 bottles of Champagne. There are usually three *cuvées* which make up this entire 'first pressing'. This term *cuvée* cannot be exactly translated, because it means both the yield of the series of pressings and the blend that is subsequently composed. *Cuve* is a vat, so the term *cuvée* might be interpreted both as 'vatting' (or 'the contents of the vat') and also, when referring to the final form of Champagne before it is bottled, as meaning the ultimate blend made up from the different vattings.

The later pressings yield juice that may be used in a Champagne

A round Champagne press

establishment's other wines, or else sold to other producers or be utilised for the making of specifically ordered Champagnes, such as the Buyer's Own Brands (see page 43).

It is important to realise that the amounts of wine allowed to be called "Champagne", the amounts that can be made into Coteaux Champenois, and the remainder that is destined for distillation as industrial alcohol are, each of them, subject to strict controls. This is so that the quality of the region's finest wines can never slip or be subject to unscrupulous commercial exploitation; also, the controls enable an overall balance of the region's production to be maintained (see page 35).

Fermentation

Due to the action of the wine yeasts on the sugar in the must, the grape juice is now becoming wine by the process of fermentation. It goes into a series of vats where it can be 'cleaned', or freed from various extraneous substances that might harm the ultimate wine. Thence it is poured either into wooden casks or, more frequently nowadays, into large fermentation vats, which have the advantage of being easier to clean. It is here that the wine completes the first stage of fermentation. Sometimes it is necessary to assist the process of fermentation with specially chosen yeasts or a wine that is already vigorously fermenting: this would happen if the vintage had taken place in wet weather or if other climatic conditions had impaired the start of fermentation.

The fermentation continues – ideally, with new wine, in furious agitation, as if boiling. Then, when the process of converting the sugar in the must to alcohol has been completed, the wine calms down and the colder weather causes the action of the yeasts to cease – cellar doors are opened to stop the wine working.

During the cold of the winter the wine lies quiet, but it is racked off or drained from cask or vat so as to leave any undesirable deposit behind; this takes place three times and may be followed by filtration. Then, just before the temperatures rises in the early spring, the *chef de cave* or head cellarman – who may in fact also be the wine specialist (oenologist) or even the head of the firm – composes the various *cuvées* or blends he wishes to make, selecting wines that will 'marry' into a harmonious style.

He will put aside those wines intended to make a 'vintage' in special years and allocate the finest wines to go to the luxury blends, always combining the elements that will, in time, continue the house style in the non-vintage wine. This is why each Champagne house must have enormous reserves of wine to draw on – three years' supplies at least and many establishments feel it prudent to hold up to six years' supplies, so as to be able to maintain their blends.

Bottling – and the first cork

Before they are bottled the wines are fined – this means that a substance (such as whipped egg white) is added to the wine and this substance attracts to itself any floating particles. It is then removed. Then, in the form of various blends, the wines go to the bottling line. But before bottling takes place, the *liqueur de tirage* is added to the wine. This is sugar dissolved in still Champagne, and it is added for two basic reasons.

Firstly, the added liqueur peps up the dormant yeasts in the wine, which can then revive and start up the second stage of fermentation. It is during the course of the second stage of fermentation that the yeasts produce both alcohol and the carbonic acid gas that, retained in the wine, is the sparkle. The amount of the liqueur added depends on how much natural sugar may already be in the wine – in some years, the sugar content may be high and little needs to be added.

Secondly, the *liqueur de tirage* establishes the amount of fizz that will be produced. This is measured in atmospheres; one atmosphere being the equivalent of a pressure of 15 lb per square inch (1.05 kg per square centimetre) and, as approximately 4 grammes of sugar will produce one atmosphere of pressure, the requisite *liqueur de tirage* has to be worked out in proportion to the amount of sugar already in the wine, to result in the pressure required for a fully sparkling wine. On its first cork, this pressure is 6 atmospheres (it goes down a little after the disgorging or recorking); for a *crémant* wine (see page 44) a pressure of 3.5–4.5 atmospheres is needed. Thus the wine maker calculates accordingly.

If, at the point of bottling, it is found that the yeasts already in the wine are weak or in any way unsatisfactory, a further small dose of special yeasts may be added, so that the fermentation may be successfully completed.

In the spring, and before the second stage of fermentation starts, the wine goes into bottle and the first cork is inserted. In former times this was a whole cork, which was held in place by a metal clip (an *agrafe*) fastened on to the square flange below the lip of the bottle.

Today it is more likely that a crown cork will be clipped over the rounded flange. A crown cork is made of metal and lined with plastic, with a thin layer of cork which comes in contact with the wine. The metal cover, similar to that of any soda water bottle, is pressed over the bottle lip, to secure the closure. It is called a 'crown cork' because the uneven edge gives it the vague appearance of a coronet. Inside the crown cork, up against the layer of cork, is a small plastic receptacle like a tiny pot. This is to receive the deposit that will ultimately slide down into it.

Until very recently crown corks were despised by many establishments, and certainly some that were used when they were experimenting with this type of seal were unsatisfactory: occasionally they even imparted an alien smell and taste to the wine. Nowadays it is unlikely that anyone in a blind tasting would be able to pick out a Champagne that had passed the initial stages of its life sealed by a crown cork, but some houses still refuse to use them. However, the fact that crown corks cut costs is important, as is the fact that they are easier to sterilise than ordinary corks: even the most seemingly impeccable

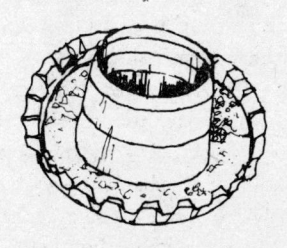

A crown cork

natural cork can have flaws. Moreover there are not as many imperfect bottles of Champagne to be found now that crown corks have been generally accepted – although the proportion was always small, it has been reduced yet further. The crown cork is here to stay, although the ordinary cork is still in use for very large bottles.

The bottles then go down to the deep cellars where they are laid on their sides and arranged in precisely stacked rows, often dozens of yards deep, in embrasures in the chalk, with lathes separating the layers. A properly laid bin of this kind should be so secure that one can walk on the top row (at a height of five feet) or, if necessary, pull out a single bottle (perhaps because of a break) from the bottom row without disturbing the others round it.

Breakages are not frequent these days, but in former times visitors to cellars would be issued with fencing masks to protect their faces against the flying glass from bottles exploding during this period of secondary fermentation. The pressure builds up inside the bottle and it is at this stage that the wine acquires its retained sparkle, known as the *prise de mousse*.

The bottles stay on their sides (*sur lattes* – on the lathes) for varying times: the legal minimum requirement is one year for non-vintage (*sans année*) and three for vintage (*millesimé*), but reputable houses will give their wines longer periods of maturation, depending on their individual character (and it should be remembered that the wine is six months old before it is bottled).

After this, it is necessary to get rid of any sludge or deposit that will, inevitably, have gone into the bottle, because the wine cannot now be filtered – after bottling it stays all its life in the one bottle. To do this, the bottles are put into slots in stands (*pupitres*), which are rather like slightly slanted easels; they rest necks down and there is usually a splash of white paint on the bottom of the punt (the indentation at the base). Then, every day, the *remueurs* or riddlers come round and, taking hold of the base of two bottles at a time, they shake them vigorously from side to side and also rotate them; this double action turns the wine round both sideways and lengthways, thereby flinging the sediment – which can be either of a greasy type or very fine, like dust – towards the neck and the cork. The riddler will give the bottles a small turn on leaving them and also increase the angle at which they lie so that, after a period that can take anything from six weeks to three months (according to the character of the sediment in the wine), the bottle will have been turned right round and will be resting upside down, the sediment having slid and been shaken down onto the cork. Unbelievable as it may seem, when one looks at the flickering hands of the *remueurs* and hears the clacking, like giant castanets, as they move along the *pupitres*, a skilled man will shake up to 40,000 in a day and turn up to 100,000 bottles! In many

A remueur turning the bottles in a pupitre

houses a magnum is the largest bottle handled by the *remueurs*, but some can actually manage jeroboams, and at least one man can handle even larger sizes. Extraordinary to the view, these giant bottles rest in the ordinary-sized *pupitres*, bulging upwards from the slots.

When so much can be mechanised today, it is little wonder that experiments have been made with devices whereby *remuage* can be carried out faster and by fewer workers. In Catalonia, where huge amounts of sparkling wine are made, following the Champagne process, the upended bottles are put into octagonal-based metal frames, several dozens at a time; the frames are then rotated, swinging the bottles around as the centre of gravity shifts according to the plane of the base. Only two workmen are needed to do this and they do not have to be particularly skilled to turn the frames. The deposit apparently swings round and, within a much shorter time than it would take a *remueur* to work, settles on the first cork of the wine.

The device seems to work satisfactorily in Catalonia, although wine makers there do also follow the traditional process of *remuage*. But the Champagne houses, although some have tried the appliance, are reluctant to abandon the process of *remuage* by hand. Of course, it is easier to keep rigid control of quality if some skilled and experienced worker is watching individual bottles day by day, month by month; the variations in the amount and type of deposit thrown in certain years can be great and require variations in handling – some deposits cling tight and are very hard to shake and turn. Obviously, it is preferable to do this by hand – if the pair of hands can still be found that can work at a rate that will not make the price of the bottle too high for the market.

But labour problems afflict Champagne, as they do other wine regions, and mechanical shaking and rotating has to be considered for the future (like mechanical grape picking). There will be changes in riddling for all but the most expensive wines, but I cannot say what form of machine-processing will be necessary for this task. It is possible that the special type of deposit that the wines throw in Champagne will require an individual type of machine to deal with this. Champagne has pioneered wine production before and may well have to again, within the next few years.

After this, the bottles are again stored, upside down or *sur les pointes*, each resting on its cork. The necks of bottles above the bottom row fit into the punts of those underneath and the rows slope slightly backwards. They look extraordinary, as if they would topple over but, coated in mould and cobwebbed dust, they can stay like this for many years. This maturation while the wine is on its first cork can be very slow, so that a guest in Champagne may be offered a wine that is fifty years old or more – but it will have remained all this time on its first cork in the cellars, and the second cork will go in only just before the wine is to be served. Sometimes only a stopper will seal the bottle for an hour or two.

Disgorging, Dosage and the Second Cork

When the wine is required for consumption, the upside-down bottles are brought up to receive their second corks. In this process, known as *dégorgement*, the first cork is removed, taking away with it the deposit stuck to the underside of the cork. Some firms still occasionally do this 'à *la volée*', the old traditional way, whereby the disgorger unclips the *agrafe*, eases out the cork and, by both strength and skill, prevents all the wine from rushing out. Students of the wine trade who go on the Champagne Academy course usually have to learn this method, for which one needs large, strong hands. If the head of a

Bottles stored sur les pointes

firm happens to be showing guests round and the *dégorgeurs* include some elderly workers who remember him as a beginner, they may well dare him to join the line and show that he can still demonstrate his skill! The more up-to-date way, however, is to freeze a section of the upended bottle neck, so that when the cork comes out it takes with it the sediment, frozen in a pellet of ice, which has collected in the small receptacle within the crown cork.

Before the second cork is inserted, the *dosage* tops up the bottle. This dose, which is a little sugar dissolved in wine, is necessary because the wine by now will have consumed all its natural sugar and be bone dry – far too dry for most tastes. According to the amount of residual sugar in the wine, the amount of sweetening permitted by the *dosage* in the five categories is as follows:

Brut: the term used may sometimes be '*nature*'. The wine may receive up to 2 per cent sweetening, but many houses use less, perhaps about 1.5 per cent. This results in a really dry wine. A *brut* that is completely without *dosage* is very dry indeed, but with certain finely-made wines the withholding of any *dosage* can be highly successful, as long as all the other conditions are right.

Extra-dry or **Extra sec:** between 1.5 per cent and 2.5 per cent of liqueur are added, producing wines that most people would find acceptably dry.

Sec: between 2 per cent and 4 per cent of liqueur may be added and this sort of wine will seem slightly sweet to many British drinkers. The *sec* category is often referred to as '*goût américain*'.

Demi-sec: this may have between 4 per cent and 6 per cent of liqueur and would certainly seem sweet. Interestingly, it perpetuates a tradition by being known as '*goût français*'.

Doux: more than 6 per cent of liqueur may be added, producing a category of wine that was scornfully described as "jam" by one wine merchant. But, with some adroitly balanced wines, the result – as with Roederer's magnificent 'Rich' – merely seems additionally fruity to the point of being luscious.

Before World War II demand was chiefly for *sec* and *demi-sec* wines, but now the category *brut* is of paramount importance, especially in export markets. However, most houses produce a range of Champagnes, and certain markets have established preferences for the sweeter wines that are made.

After the *dosage*, the second cork is inserted by means of a machine. If you see the chunk that is the undriven cork, it seems impossible that it can be forced into the narrow neck of the bottle. On top of this cork goes a metal disc (*la plaque*) to prevent the wire muzzle (*le muselet de fil de fer*) biting into it in the way that the *agrafe* does on the first cork. Then the muzzle itself goes over the cork, and the loop on it is twisted round to secure it. Although wire has been used on Champagne bottles for at least 170 years, string or thread was also used and, because it became moist with wine, the rats in the cellars used to enjoy gnawing it – which is at least one reason why metal foil capsules were used early on to protect the fastening. The length of the capsule on the Champagne bottle is said to have originated because, in former times, some deposit might remain attached to the neck and the capsule hid this; also, if a bottle had not been completely topped up, the capsule concealed the gap. The bottles receive a final brisk twirl and twist – an Indian-club-like twiddle – to ensure that the *dosage* is well mixed and, after a rest period, they will go to be 'dressed' – that is, labelled, packed and despatched. Every stage of a bottle's progress is thus supervised and regulated, and knowledge of even a little of this indicates why it is uneconomic to devote so much attention to any wine that is other than very good – and that will please when it is opened.

The Still Wines

Until August 1974 the still wines of the Champagne region were known as 'still Champagnes' or, in the singular, *'Champagne nature'*. They achieved a certain fame, mainly because it was very difficult to obtain them except in the Champagne region. The Champenois were anxious lest these wines should be exported, gasified and subsequently sold as 'Champagne'. At certain periods their export was prohibited.

Since 1974, however, the still wines have been entitled to their own *appellation contrôlée*,* 'Coteaux Champenois'. They are, however, subject to controls as strict as those that safeguard the sparkling wines. They must all – white, red and pink – start off by complying with all the legal requirements of a Champagne: vines, method of cultivation, density of growing, method of pruning, maximum yield, system of making into wine (traditionally established), and anything else that applies to the wines that are to go to make Champagne.

These still wines may only be made as a proportion of the total yield of the Champagne vineyard. This is decreed by the C.I.V.C., and any grapes left over after the legal amounts have been destined to be made into Champagne or Coteaux Champenois cannot be utilised for the still wines, but must be disposed of for distillation into industrial alcohol.

The Coteaux Champenois are picked, pressed and undergo their initial fermentation just like Champagne. They are racked, fined and filtered and eventually bottled; sometimes the *agrafe* and first type of cork are used when they go into bottle (they must be bottled in the region), because they do occasionally display a liveliness traditional in the region, but otherwise they are still wines. Some are sealed with an ordinary cork, some with a crown cork (see page 29). They must bear the *appellation contrôlée*, and the words "Coteaux Champenois" on the labels must be in letters at least as large as those of any other descriptive matter.

The majority of Coteaux Champenois are white; the Chardonnay makes fine dry white wines, and there is a definite place for these as a wine to drink with certain foods. However, there are a few red

* For definition, see page 51.

Coteaux Champenois; Bouzy is probably the best-known, because of its 'comic' name, but it is worth mentioning that the other red growths, such as those of Cumières and Ambonnay (see page 44), produce wines as individual as Bouzy, and they should certainly be tried by visitors to the region.

Many of the great Champagne houses now produce still wines as well as the sparkling ones. They usually made some, anyway, for personal use, but nowadays the demand for Coteaux Champenois – which are never cheap – has encouraged sales on a commercial scale, especially when stocks of Champagne are well maintained after a succession of good vintages.

At the same time there are definitely some establishments who do not think that this aspect of wine-making in the Champagne region is ideal: "Why return to the days of our ancestors?" objected the director of one great house. "For domestic use, a little still wine – yes. But the glory of Champagne is the artistry of the blend and the fact that the wine has its heavenly sparkle! Why make this retrograde step at a time when it is so easy for the public to buy a good dry white wine from other vineyards of France?"

Laurent Perrier, who are particularly prominent in the still wine business, do not agree with this view, because they feel it is this very antiquity of the tradition of still wines that merits attention. But the wine lover must make up his own mind.

Other Local Drinks

Ratafia

This is an odd drink, and the Shorter Oxford Dictionary's definition: "A cordial or liqueur flavoured with almonds, or peach- apricot- or cherry kernels" should not be relied on. In fact ratafia was, in former times, made in many of the regions where wine was made, and it was flavoured with various fruits, herbs, nuts, berries and even chocolate; it was used for medicinal purposes (including being a draught recommended for women in labour), and as an antidote against various forms of poison and snake-bite.

But ratafia got its name and began its life as a simpler beverage. It was the drink taken to seal an agreement of two people in front of a lawyer: they signified their assent by consenting to the Latin pronouncement "*De quibus est res, ut rata fiat, publicum fecimus instrumentum"*, which means, in general terms, "Concerning the matter in hand, we have put our hands to a public deed, so that the business is confirmed". The lawyer then poured out the '*rata fiat*' or ratafia, which he and the parties concerned shared.

Sometimes ratafia seems, from references, to have been a non-alcoholic fruit-based drink, but in many instances it was clearly a strong drink. In Congreve's *The Way of the World*, the hero, Mirabell, mentions it in connection with "orange-brandy, aniseed, cinnamon, citron and Barbados waters, together with ratafia and the most noble spirit of clary". It does usually appear to have been a sweetish beverage, and the survival of the ratafia biscuit – the round, miniature macaroon, traditional as decoration on the top of English trifles – indicates that it was generally a small portion of something sweet and/or fruity, taken as a between-times refreshment. There are dozens of recipes for ratafia drinks in the household books of the early American colonists, utilising walnuts, angelica, pomegranates, orange flowers, even 'usquebaugh' (whisky), violets and coffee. Today, however, the only surviving ratafia seems to be that which is still made in Champagne.

The process for making ratafia is straightforward: the freshly-pressed grape juice is combined with brandy, Cognac being used for the best results. As the addition of the spirit prevents the juice from undergoing the process of fermentation, the mixture consists of grape juice and brandy; this, after a year or so of maturation in wood, is bottled and then offered for sale.

Ratafia is an excellent any-time drink or apéritif, as long as people are not silly about insisting on a bone dry drink before a meal (very few truly like such a thing, especially those inhabitants of northern, chilly, rheumatically-inclined countries). It is fruity rather than syrupy, and should be served chilled.

Marc

When the grapes have been subjected to the final pressing that will give juice suitable for using as wine, the remainder of the debris of pips, skins and stalks is squeezed harder to yield a liquid that can then be distilled. This is marc (pronounced 'mah'). There are various types, made in the various different wine regions. The style of the particular marc depends on the type of residue from which the liquid was originally distilled and, even more, on how and for how long this spirit is matured.

In Champagne, it seems that the firms who distil (the best-known is Goyard, at Ay) sell some of the spirit to various Champagne establishments, who then do their own maturing in oak – often using smaller casks than the usual ample size used for wine. The distillers also keep some for themselves, and then market the spirit when they consider it to be mature. The stills, I am informed, can be the mobile or travelling type, so that distilling can be carried out in the country as well as at the distillery. In Champagne they also are said to employ a type of still peculiar to the region, called an *alembic à vases*, whereby the heated vapour passes through three vessels or 'pots' and then goes through a rectifying or correcting column, before emerging as a spirit that must then be aged.

Marc de Champagne is obviously a special type of brandy that the visitor ought to try to sample. Its style and quality will, naturally, vary, but from my own experience I think that at its best it is a delicate, lightly forceful spirit. It should be treated like any good brandy, served in a small balloon or tulip-shaped glass that can be cupped in one hand to enable the drinker to get the aroma from the slightly warmed spirit. Some experts consider that a marc de Champagne made from the skins of Chardonnay grapes is usually better than one made from the skins of the Pinot, but few restaurateurs will know – or say – anything about the source or foundation of their marc de Champagne. It is logical to find the marc made from the Chardonnay more *fin* – a term that cannot be translated as 'fine', but possibly signifies a delicate intensity in English – simply because our appraisal of any brandy is inevitably conditioned by our knowledge of Cognac, which is a distillate of wine made from white grapes. However, anybody able to sample several sorts of marc in Champagne should try and form an individual opinion.

Fine

A fine (pronounced 'feen') is a brandy distilled from wine. It becomes agreeably drinkable sooner than a marc and tends to be lighter, smoother and more delicate. A Fine Marne is therefore a brandy distilled from Champagne – from the still wines. The term as given here is the correct one, although many writers – including myself—have sometimes incorrectly expressed it as "Fine de la Marne".

Much depends on what the original wine was like and, as with marc, the way in which the distillation was carried out and the way in which the resulting spirit was matured. No one is likely to be able to find out much about any of these processes simply by asking whoever is selling or supplying the fine; however, the drinker's critical faculty should be concerned with the pleasure the spirit bestows – its subtlety of aroma, its smoothness and delicacy on the palate and its cleanness of 'finish'. Do not attempt to compare a Fine Marne with any other good brandy – appraise it on its own merits. It can give great pleasure.

4
The Wine in Bottle

The vineyards in the Champagne region are divided into what can be tiny plots, split between thousands of proprietors. The great Champagne establishments own few plots, some of them having what are virtually only personal vineyards, while others own no vineyards at all. They are primarily concerned with the making of the wine and the handling of it once it is made, so that their work – and their capital outlay – would be enormously increased if they were also substantial proprietors.

The Business Arrangements

The owners of the scraps of vineyard – some of them shippers and the rest the huge number of peasant proprietors – often possess allotment-sized holdings; it is common for a tiny site to be less than a hectare*, even as small as a quarter of an acre or 0.61 ha. The holdings may be dotted about, at some distant from each other. This can be a great advantage to the owner, who thereby has several plots from which to make up his wine. Many of those who own vineyards arrange to run those belonging to other proprietors, which can be useful if an owner has another business to occupy him as well. A vineyard must be supervised all through the year and although it can, if big enough, provide a living for the owner, he is unlikely to be able to spend both the money and time, including paying the work force, in making the wine as well.

The shippers (*négociants*) have often established relationships extending through several generations in buying the grapes of particular owners. Therefore any changes in a vineyard, brought about by plots being linked through marriage, purchase or simply because someone

---

* A hectare, usually abbreviated to 'ha.', is 2.47 acres

wants to try new methods or experiment with procedures, may well be referred to and discussed with the men who, at the end of the vintage, will be using the produce of that vineyard to make the wine. This is another reason why, in addition to the huge installations at the headquarters of the great Champagne houses, there are many more presshouses out in the country, so that as little time as possible is wasted in handling the grapes from the time when they are picked. These *vendangeoirs* often have accommodation for the vintagers as well; they must be well housed and fed if they are to complete their hard work satisfactorily.

A grower who actually makes his own wine is a *récoltant-manipulant*; a member of a Champagne house (or the establishment itself) engaged in processing the wine and then selling it is a *négociant manipulant*. It is not permitted for anyone to make or process Champagne in a presshouse outside the defined area, even if the grapes have been grown within it. Nor can even the most important establishments buy grapes just as and where they wish; only by belonging to the Comité Interprofessionnel du Vin de Champagne (see page 22) is it possible to purchase grapes. However, members have to obtain the requisite permits to buy – this is because the C.I.V.C. protects the growers by sharing out the most sought-after produce as fairly as possible. The Institut National des Appellations d'Origine, with which the C.I.V.C. has a close relationship, is the body that can determine whether or not to allow a particular plot to be used to plant vines for making Champagne: it is strict about insisting that the site has been traditionally used for vines since before 1927 and that it is wholly suitable for the production of quality wine. Local authorities are called in to establish this.

The Grandes Marques

Reference is frequently made to such-and-such a Champagne as being a '*grande marque*'. Because the term implies superiority – whether as a quality wine or because of its commercial importance – it is wise to exercise tact in using it. There is, in fact, no formal list of 'members', the *grandes marques* are not an official body, nor will the C.I.V.C. pronounce as to who is and who is not a member; even quite a large house might not claim that they are a *grande marque*, however fine their wine. Conversely, some of those who are generally admitted as having a right to the title are smallish (although, with its required reserves, no Champagne house can ever be described as truly small).

The correct French title of this informal association – they organise the annual 'Champagne Academy' study sessions for wine trade students, who spend time working in the great houses so that they have practical and detailed experience of every stage of the wine's production – is *"Liste de Grandes Marques"*; if there were a defined and limited membership, like that of a club, the title would read *"Liste des . . ."* Firms who are generally associated in this way with the term are: Ayala, Bollinger, Veuve Clicquot-Ponsardin, Deutz & Geldermann, Heidsieck Monopole, Charles Heidsieck, Irroy, Krug, Lanson, Mercier, Moët et Chandon, G.H. Mumm, Perrier-Jouët, Piper Heidsieck, Pol Roger, Pommery & Greno, Roederer, Ruinart (the oldest house still in business, now belonging to Moët), and Taittinger. The British and the American markets attach a certain value – snob appeal – to the use of the phrase *grande marque*, so the words tend to be used more in these countries and are sometimes claimed by firms additional to the above list.

Types of Champagne

Non-Vintage

The bulk of all Champagne is non-vintage. Each establishment has its own idea as to the style of wine it wishes to make. Many make more than one type of non-vintage, which can be more or less expensive. There is a definite and perceptible difference between the style of the houses, some making fullish wines, others light ones. Everyone should try as many as possible, so as to form preferences for, say, Champagnes that are good as mid-morning drinks, or those that are excellent supper wines; those that are delicately brisk apéritifs; those that are fruity enough to partner certain foods; and those that are fuller and slightly soft for drinking at the end of a meal, perhaps on a special occasion.

The liking for dryish drinks these days causes many people to overlook the great sweet Champagnes. Yet these, full and opulent without ever being cloying, can be marvellous at the end of a dinner or, even, for a reviving drink at the end of a hard, cold day. The late Philip Harben would thoughtfully offer dinner guests a choice of either Roederer Dry or Rich. As a leisurely apéritif, the Rich can be a wonderful refreshment, as well as being excellent after a meal.

Buyer's Own Brands

As well as the well-known names of the range of wines produced by the Champagne houses, there are what are called the B.O.B. wines – 'Buyer's Own Brands'. These are wines made to the requirements of special customers, such as great hotel groups, luxury restaurants and reputable wine merchants, plus a few private individuals – for example Baron Philippe de Rothschild, who has his own *marque* of Champagne. These wines are usually somewhat cheaper than the known and advertised brands, simply because they do not have to bear the cost of publicity and marketing, but this does not mean that they are necessarily inferior in quality: the great house of Trouillard, for example, which makes Champagne De Venoge, including the luxury blend Vin des Princes, also makes the B.O.B. of one of the greatest of London's hotel groups and the 'house wine' of several respected City merchants. If you ever want to trace a B.O.B. back to its source, the code number on the label will enable you to do this (see page 51). Each Champagne is identifiable.

Vintage

A vintage Champagne is the wine of a single year. Not every year results in a wine which is worth keeping apart in this way, as the climatic problems of the Champagne vineyard make the non-vintage wines, with their continuity of quality, the backbone of the business. Even with a vintage Champagne it is legally permitted to correct any deficiencies in the vintage with the addition of up to 20 per cent of another wine from another vintage (which will have been kept under pressure in reserve for this possible use).

Vintage Champagne possesses the individuality of its year as well as that of its establishment. Usually, it is considered to be at its peak when between seven and twelve years from its vintage date. But this, of course, applies to wines that have received their second cork; they age rather fast after this and although some people – myself included – like the rather softened, deeper gold and somewhat honeyed style of old Champagnes, which may have lost some of their vivacity, this is a very personal taste indeed. It is generally not worth keeping Champagne so long that you risk finding only an old, tired wine when you open the bottle. Wines kept on their first cork, in the cellars of their birthplace, of course remain in fine form for much longer, but you will not find these outside the Champagne region.

Rosé

Pink Champagne or *rosé* is mostly non-vintage, but some vintage pink is made. There are two methods whereby it acquires its colour: if a blend of black and white grapes is used to make it, then the black grapes, if suitably ripe, will be left in contact with the 'must' long enough for the pigments in their skins to tint the wine. Or the wine may be blended with certain specified red wines of the region: those of Bouzy are certainly the best-known, because of the name, but there are others, including those of Ambonnay, Ay, Cumières, Dizy, Rilly, Verzenay and Villedommange. But pink Champagne is tricky to make and, although a fine vintage pink can be excellent, it is as a silver-gold wine that the Champenois see the real glory of their region.

Blanc de blancs and Blanc de noirs

Blanc de blancs is a wine made solely from white grapes. *Blanc de noirs* is one made from black grapes. Because of the unsound 'expertise' of James Bond, many people think a *blanc de blancs* is 'the best' Champagne. It is nothing of the kind. It is a very light, zippy wine, often possessing elegance and finesse, and there is a time and a place for it – usually as an apéritif or to drink early in the day. A *blanc de noirs*, made from black grapes, will not often be found outside the region. It is generally fruity and full, with a pronounced bouquet – perhaps a wine for accompanying food.

Crémant

In recent years, a new category of Champagne has been produced by some houses – that of *crémant*. This term has nothing to do with the village Cramant, but refers to a less vigorous *mousse* (sparkle) in the wine. This varies, usually being between 3.5 and 4 or 4.5 atmospheres (whereas a fully *mousseux* wine has about 5.6 atmospheres) but, as far as I can discover, there is no rigidity of control about this. In some wine regions, where wines of varying degrees of sparkle are made, the term *pétillant* can describe anything from a wine with quite a pronounced sparkle to one which is only very slightly fizzy.

Of course, in the days before much was known about the chemistry of wine, there would have been considerable variations in the amount of bubbles in Champagne, and it is reasonable to assume that some makers would have had customers who preferred wines that were slightly less fizzy than others (the wine was vivaceous anyway, until it got old and tended to become flat). But the exact control of the vivacity and the ability to establish its amount of vigour in the initial stages of production were skills that could only have been guessed at until the nineteenth century.

It is not usually at all easy to see the difference between a Champagne that is *crémant* and one that is fully *mousseux* until they can actually be poured and compared side by side, and even then you may have to peer hard at the two glasses. The bubbles will be as tiny and fast-rising in a *crémant* wine as in one that is fully sparkling, and in every way a quality *crémant* can be appraised like another fine Champagne. Perhaps it may be easiest to feel the difference on the palate, when the *crémant* will tend to feel gentler and less tingling. In some ways, the slightly lower pressure is particularly revealing of the quality of the wine, because its basic character is less concealed by the liveliness of the *mousse*. Personally, I find a good *crémant* a beautiful wine; one such as the *crémant* of George Goulet makes an interesting variation in Champagne drinking and, perhaps, is an easier wine to accompany some kinds of food than a fully sparkling one (see page 88).

Single vineyard wines

Single growth Champagnes are the most interesting newcomers to the market. These are the wines of single vineyards, most notably those in or in the vicinity of Ay and Bouzy. As might be expected, they have great individuality. Some lovers of Champagne find that many of them lack the balance and interest that the blends of the great houses have perfected, but there are several producers, notably those of Bouzy-Barancourt at Bouzy, and Collery at Ay, who make wines I find superb by any standards. They can never be cheap, but they should certainly be tried.

De luxe Champagnes

Luxury Champagnes are, quite simply, the wines that certain houses consider to be the very finest that they can make. Some are vintage, some non-vintage, some *blancs de blancs*, others not, and there is at least one *rosé*. They are superb and highly individual – indeed, their individuality is very marked; a comparative tasting of some illuminated in detail to me the different ideas of perfection that are held by the great establishments. It is only fair to add, however, that some houses – notably Krug and Pol Roger – assert that their regular vintage or non-vintage wines are the finest that they can achieve and so they do not make a luxury blend.

Some, as with Veuve Clicquot's Grande Dame, follow a blend actually evolved by Madame Clicquot for her guests from vineyards owned by her. Some, such as Bollinger's Vieilles Vignes, make use of ungrafted vines and others, like the Bollinger Tradition 'R.D.' (the initials stand for *récemment dégorgé* – recently disgorged), provide a vintage wine with much longer maturation than is usual.

Moët's Dom Pérignon is certainly the most famous; Moët own the Hautvillers Abbey site (see page 11), and this Champagne was evolved, with business courage, at the time of the between-wars depression, so as to evoke interest in Champagne, in a bottle of similar shape to that used in the seventeenth century.

Today there are quite a number of these de luxe wines available outside the region as well as in it. Among these beautiful wines are: Ruinart Dom Ruinart; Perrier-Jouët Belle Époque and Blason de France; Laurent Perrier Cuvée Grand Siècle; Taittinger Comtes de Champagne; Louis Roederer Cristal Brut; Heidsieck Dry Monopole Cuvée Diamant Bleu; Canard-Duchêne Charles VII Brut; Charles Heidsieck Royal; Piper-Heidsieck Florens-Louis; De Venoge Vin des Princes; Mercier Réserve de l'Empéreur; G.H. Mumm René Lalou; Deutz & Geldermann Cuvée William Deutz; Irroy Chasteau de Irroy.

The Bottle

Sizes of Champagne bottles are as follows: quarter or nip; half bottle; imperial pint, which might be described as a three-quarter bottle size; bottle; magnum, which is 2 bottles; Jeroboam – 2 magnums or 4 bottles; Rehoboam – 6 bottles; Methusaleh – 8 bottles; Salmanezar – 12 bottles; Balthazar – 16 bottles; Nebuchadnezzar – 20 bottles.

Not only are the large sizes impressively big, they are also very heavy: the glass has to be extra-thick so as to resist the pressure from the carbon dioxide inside. The standard bottle itself is the biggest and heaviest of all wine bottles of standard size – 80 centilitres. The most important sizes today are the bottle, half, quarter and magnum. Except for the half bottle and magnum, wine in smaller or larger bottles will generally have been decanted from bottles or magnums after *remuage* by the process known as *transvasage* (transfer under pressure), to avoid the wine losing its effervescence. This is a practical measure, for it is extremely difficult to shake and turn any bottle larger than a magnum, and it would be a waste of time to subject quarter bottles to *remuage* (see page 30); also, the wastage if a large bottle should split would be considerable.

The imperial pint, which may be referred to in France as a '*médium*' or '*impérial*',* used to be popular in Victorian times and occasionally nowadays pleas are made for a revival of its use. Sir Winston Churchill liked the size, saying that "A half bottle is not enough for me, but a bottle is too much for my wife – she says if I drink it all I become bad-tempered." The magnum is generally considered to be the size that will result in the finest wine, and Patrick Forbes explains why: "Air is the enemy of Champagne. Now, of the three sizes of bottle upon which *transvasage* is never practised – the half-bottle, the bottle and the magnum – the magnum is the one that contains the smallest air-bubble in relation to the liquid in contains, and the one, consequently, that produces the most perfect Champagne."

Because any roughness inside the bottle would increase the liveliness in the wine and thus risk the bottle bursting, the production of bottles has to be of a high standard. Today the lip of the bottle is shaped according to whether the producers are going to use an *agrafe* or a crown cork on it: for the *agrafe*, the flange below the lip is squared off so that the clip can fit over it and hold tight. For the crown cork, the flange is rounded and narrower.

Nowadays the majority of bottles are green in colour – a dark tone of glass is protection for the wine against the light. In the nineteenth century, however, they were brown. When Madame Roederer put her luxury *cuvée* into clear glass there were many heads shaken – but, correctly stored, Roederer Cristal is invariably a superb wine.

The shape of bottles can vary, especially for the luxury wines. Some firms, such as Moët et Chandon, use a narrow-necked bottle, like those of former times, for their Dom Pérignon; Clicquot-Ponsardin use the *bombé* curvaceous bottle for their Grande Dame. However, the majority of bottles are the standard shape. Also, although an unusually shaped bottle can attract attention effectively, it may be difficult to bin.

Corks

As might be expected with a wine as complex as Champagne, the cork of each bottle is itself a small but important piece of craftsman-

* Not to be confused with the Bordeaux *impériale*, which holds 8 bottles.

ship. It has to resist the pressure inside (which is equivalent to the pressure in the tyre of a London double-decker bus), and it has to keep the wine without imparting any alien smell or flavour. Only the very finest segments of matured and treated bark from the cork oak will do, but a cork made solely from one single chunk of cork eventually became both too expensive and too scarce to be practical. Between the wars they developed what was termed a 'laminated' cork, by sticking several suitable slivers of cork, cut lengthways, together. Later still, corks were composed of four sections, two cut lengthways to form the top and two, underneath these, cut and glued on crosswise. This four-piece cork had the economic advantage that only the two circular sections, those in contact with the wine, needed to be of the finest hard quality. Obviously, a cork that is too soft might not be able to withstand the pressure of the bottle neck and of the wine, so that it might either admit air or simply slide out of the bottle, however well secured.

A still later development was the evolution of the *agglomèré* cork: this consists of a series of circular rounds, glued together. The top quality section is that immediately in contact with the wine: this face of the cork is referred to as *la tranche* or *le miroir*. The other layers are of lesser quality up towards the 'mushroom' part; this mushroom is made up of fragments or crumb-like pieces of cork, bonded together, and if you examine an unused *agglomèré* cork you will notice that this speckled section represents a substantial proportion of the whole. A few houses, such as Krug, refuse to employ the *agglomèré* type of cork at all, while others use it merely for the non-vintage wines. All those who insist on the more expensive types of cork aver that they can detect differences in the wines stoppered with the various kinds, and they hold that only whole sections of cork are fit to stopper the finest wines. But it seems fair comment that very few members of the public would be aware of such a difference, although they certainly would notice any increase in the price of the bottle of wine.

The use of the crown cork (*bouchon couronne*), which is the metal cap that is clipped over the top of the bottle and which has a layer of cork inside, is one of the most radical changes in the production of Champagne in recent years. It has now largely replaced the old type of first cork, fastened to the bottle with the *agrafe* or metal clip, as first cork for non-vintage wines. Even as recently as ten years ago, many firms expressed horror at the idea of using such a substitute, and experiments seemed to confirm the theory held by large numbers

THE WINE IN BOTTLE · 49

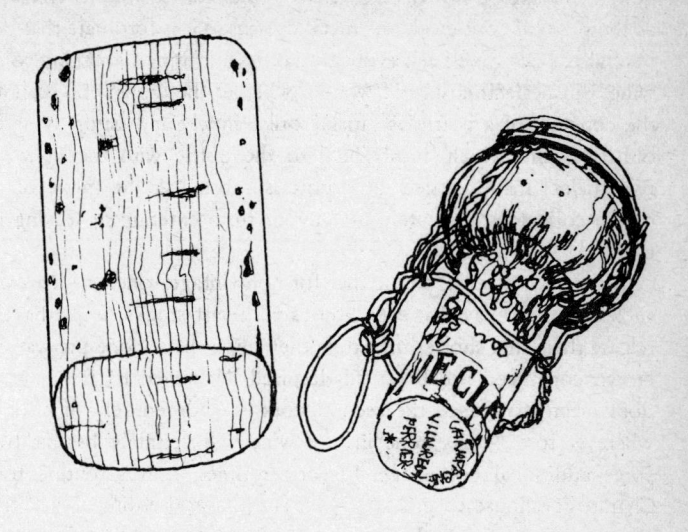

Champagne corks before and after use – vintage (above) and non-vintage (below)

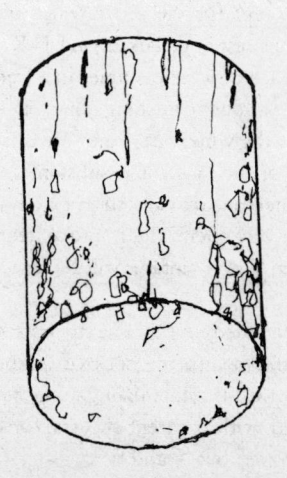

of even the most progressive establishments that the contact of plastic with the wine was utterly deleterious. Yet it was found necessary to have a tiny cup of plastic held inside the crown cork to catch and hold the shaken-down deposit, as it would not be able to cling just to the sliver of cork inside the metal crown, so it is fortunate that now neutral plastics have been evolved that do not impart anything to the wine. But perfectionists still wonder whether the crown cork can age the contents of a bottle as satisfactorily, slowly and naturally as the old-style cork which, firmly held to the bottle with the *agrafe*, is nonetheless made entirely of a porous substance: the metal of the crown cork does absolutely bar any air from entering or leaving the bottle.

Personally, it seems to me that for non-vintage wines, which are in such demand today that even houses with vast stocks simply have to release them in a shorter time than they might have done pre-war, the crown cork need not be at all despised. However, its frequent use does mean that, once the second cork – made entirely of cork, in whatever form – has gone in, the wine will certainly benefit from some additional bottle age. In former times, it was routine for a Champagne house to give six months or more 'settling down' time after the disgorging and recorking, before they would send the wine away; nowadays they simply may not be able to afford this extra maturation. The same applies to merchants: before World War II, even the most inexpensive non-vintage Champagne would be given several months' rest in a British cellar before customers could buy it. Today, such 'landing age' is uneconomic except for the finest wines and by the owners of the biggest – and cheapest – cellars in the U.K. The rental represented by the space one case of wine occupies in a London cellar in 1979 is around 50p a week! Such 'keeping charges' can't always be added to the retail price of the wine, but if they are not they cut down the profit of shipper and/or merchant in a substantial way. This is why, if the domestic consumer can manage to put away even a few bottles of Champagne after buying them, the improvement due to the additional maturation on even a non-vintage will be beneficial and notable.

To some people – not, to my knowledge, the Champenois – the plastic stopper, with grooves to wedge it into the neck of the bottle, is the next stage in the attempt to cut costs while maintaining quality. These plastic stoppers have been used, with apparent success, for some sparkling wines other than Champagne, but – and it is a significant qualifying phrase – these wines have, in my experience, been those that would only have been in bottle a short time anyway, and those that are not intended to benefit by bottle-age after the second cork goes in.

Only time will indicate whether improved types of plastic can, in some instances, replace the use of cork for fine wines maturing long-term in bottle.

Champagne Labels

Everything about Champagne is subject to controls. There is a constant surveillance on the quality of the wines and also on the way in which they are presented to the public. Many interesting traditions are perpetuated by the way the bottle is 'dressed': for example, the capsule, which is unusually long compared with the capsules covering the corks of ordinary table wines, is like this because, in the days before scrupulously efficient *remuage* and modern machinery ensured that the deposit was completely removed from the bottle with the first cork, some sludge or deposit might still remain in the neck of the bottle. The extra-long capsule would hide this from the purchaser.

Champagne is the only French wine that possesses an *appellation d'origine contrôlée* (signifying its place of origin, vines, method of cultivation, maximum yield and procedures of vinification, plus minimum degree of alcohol) which does not have to state the circumstance of its having an A.C. on its label. The words "Vin de Champagne" or "Champagne" suffice.

But whatever the wine is named and whether the producers offer it for sale under one of their own house names, or the name registered by them as a *sous marque*, or as produce of a firm that they own, there is a code number and letters on every label that enable it to be traced to its source if necessary.

Each principal label on every bottle must state the following:
The word "Champagne" has to be given, printed in clear, easily-distinguishable letters.
The name of the brand or the name of the establishment responsible for offering the wine must be clearly shown.
The registered number of the brand, bestowed by the C.I.V.C., must appear – even if only in small print. Each of these numbers will be preceded by one set of the following letters:

N.M. – The wine's actual name, registered as belonging to one particular *négociant manipulant*.

M.A. – Any subsidiary name that belongs to a *négociant manipulant*, or a brand name belonging to an establishment responsible for marketing Champagne that has been made by another producer, or made by a grower.

R.M. – A registered name belonging to the proprietor of a vineyard (*récoltant-manipulant*) who makes and sells his own wine.

C.M. – A registered name belonging to a co-operative of producers.

The word "Champagne" must be printed on the labels in letters at least as large as any other words thereon and, in addition, it must also appear on cases, cartons, packages, corks and capsules.

On the label the name or brand of the shipper must be given, plus the address of the person or firm responsible for making or selling the wine, the volume of wine in the bottle, the registration of the C.I.V.C. and, when necessary, the vintage date – which must also be on the cork.

Expressions such as "*Propriétaire à . . .*", "*Viticulteur à . . .*" and so on may only be used by growers who are selling the wines grown from their own vines – and nothing else.

The term "*Premier cru*" may only be used for wines coming from communes classified as 100 per cent to 90 per cent. The term "*Grand cru*" may only be used for wines coming from communes classified as 100 per cent entirely.

It is not allowed to put phrases such as "*Nature*", "*Près Reims*" (or "*Près Épernay*"), "*Cru classé*", "*Côte des Blancs*", "*Vallée de la Marne*", "*Montagne de Reims*" or any similar geographical descriptions on the label at all.

Visiting the Region

'La Champagne' – the region – is comparatively little-known. People rush through it on the big main roads en route for somewhere else; from these main roads there appears little of interest or beauty and, if your route takes you from Soissons to Reims and eastwards, it is unlikely that a single vine or vineyard will be seen! Yet much of La Champagne is beautiful: open, undulating landscape, with many woods, lakes, quiet rivers, elegant *châteaux* all but hidden behind wrought-iron gates and formal parks, villages huddled round churches that are often surprisingly big and impressive, bustling towns that retain many shop-fronts exactly as they were in the nineteenth century. The museums and works of art abound, and there are plenty of places to stay. These range from the luxurious *châteaux hôtels* out in the country to modern accommodation in the towns, from all but top class to the simple and cheap – the latter often being more interesting to the traveller who wants to explore the real France and who can speak a little French.

As the region receives a number of visitors from Germany, Belgium and Holland, as well as from Paris, the extra language – if one is spoken – tends to be German rather than English. In the Champagne establishments there will usually be people who speak English, and certainly in the larger houses the guides can cope with a wide range of languages. But even a hesitant attempt to speak French will be welcomed and appreciated. The Champenois, a northern French people, are somewhat reserved and have been toughened through the centuries of devastating wars; they are not always forthcoming towards foreigners, so the visitor who bothers to make the gesture of trying to talk to them in their own tongue will make a definite contribution to international understanding and goodwill.

Because the whole Champagne area is extensive, the use of a car

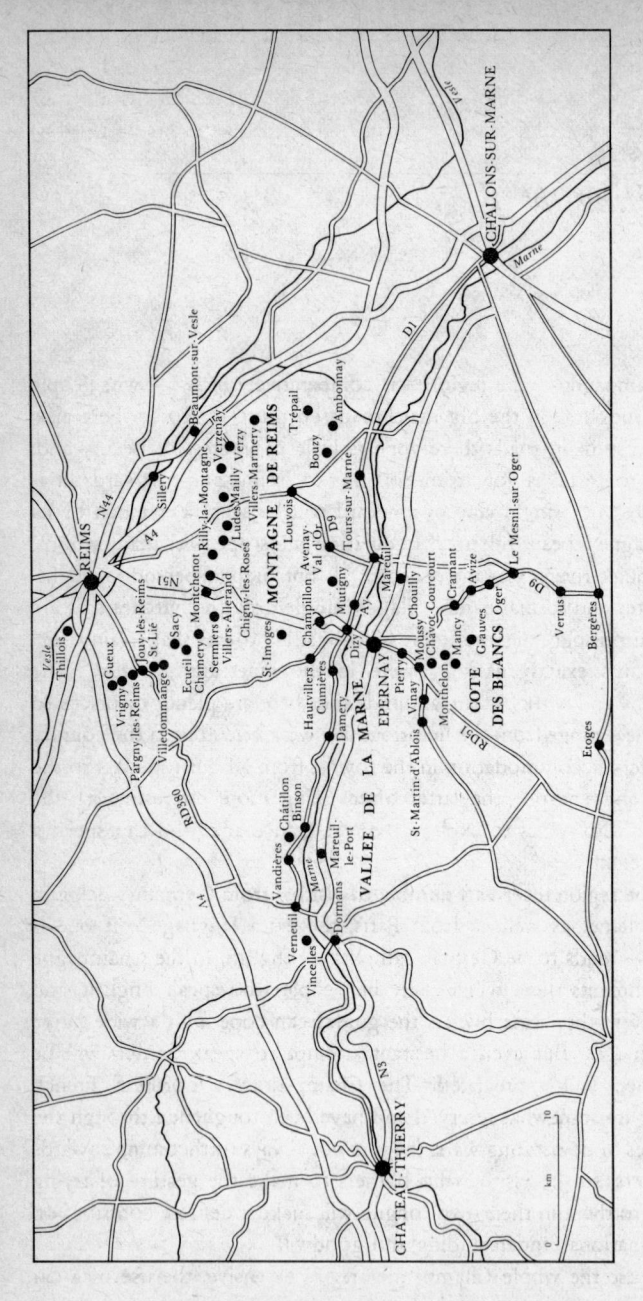

Map of the Champagne region

is really essential. It is possible to stay in either Épernay or Reims, to visit several wine establishments and take part in one of the coach tours of the neighbouring countryside organised by local tourist bureaux, but some form of independent transport is really necessary if the wine lover is to register sharp impressions of vineyards and vines. Several travel agencies organise trips to Champagne for wine enthusiasts, and these can be good value if time is very limited. Of course if a wine club or society arrange to make travel arrangements, this can be most convenient of all – the fact that Champagne is so accessible from Britain makes a visit of even a couple of days really rewarding.

Drivers who are hesitant about making an excursion across the Channel can be reassured: Champagne is easy of access both from Paris and the Channel ports, and it is a region in which even the inexperienced can drive without qualms. The roads are either the main ones, fast and generally fairly wide, or else they wind through the sort of country in which there is seldom much traffic.

Where to Base a Stay

The obvious centres are Reims and Épernay, also Troyes in the south. Reims is a big city, much developed, with good shops, parks, a variety of excellent restaurants and plenty of hotels. The great works of art are the Cathedral (with the stained glass of Marc Chagall recently added to the other windows), the adjacent Palais du Tau (which holds the treasures of the establishment), the Basilica of St. Rémi and its museum, the Chapelle Foujita (decorated by the Japanese artist of that name), and a number of other museums. In the neighbourhood are various monuments and relics of World War I that will be of great interest to students of the subject.

The Reims Champagne establishments, including many with *crayères* (see page 5), provide plenty for the wine lover to see. Anyone staying in Reims could also hire a car or taxi to go over to Épernay, so as to see something of this town, for it can be reached within half an hour by the main road. A return route might be through the forest where the odd *'faux' de Verzy* (see page 65), trees of an unusual type, are well worth seeing, as are the different vineyards passed on the way.

Épernay is a smaller town, much damaged during World War I and, therefore, containing fewer ancient monuments than Reims. But it is perhaps more obviously the centre of the Champagne trade, and it is at the junction of several of the official *'routes du Champagne'*. Here is the office of the C.I.V.C. (see page 18) and here, in the Avenue de Champagne, leading out of the main square, is the Musée du Vin de Champagne, housed in the Château Perrier, which also contains fine art exhibits. This and the Hôtel de Ville (Town Hall) were formerly private houses, the Museum belonging to the Perrier family, the Town Hall to Auban Moët.

Walk down the Avenue de Champagne and look at the many imposing edifices – in Épernay they are easy to view, whereas in Reims many such buildings are at least partly concealed at the ends of drives and behind carefully planted foliage. When families – and their staff – lived in such establishments the impression of wealth and influence must have been overwhelming. Just before the Musée de Champagne ceased to be a private house there were sixteen staff living in, all to look after the few elderly inhabitants.

The gardens and orangery of Le Trianon, belonging to Moët et Chandon, are also easy to view from the Avenue de Champagne – they were laid out by the painter Isabey in the last century, during the First Empire. Still in the Avenue is the Mercier establishment. Almost within living memory, it was considered so far out of the town that, when it was being built, the workers were said to be going "as far as Peking" when they left for their daily stint – hence its name: Château de Pékin.

Not all the buildings are of architectural importance, but a walk along the Avenue de Champagne – with the many vast wine establishments facing the substantial buildings that were formerly private dwellings, with the huge tower of Castellane rising above the river, with the realisation that one is standing above storeys of galleries 60 miles long containing millions of bottles of wine – is something that the wine lover must not miss.

Troyes was the former capital of the Province of Champagne. Today it is a bustling town, superficially modern in style and certainly somewhat noisy as a place in which to stay. But the museums and works of art are wonderful, and it is the centre of a knitting industry that has flourished since the sixteenth century. There is a museum concerned with this craft, as well as a museum of Troyes and the Champagne region, both of which are in the Hotel de Vauluisant. Also worth seeing is the unique museum devoted to the tools and work equipment of all types of craftsman. The churches display the work of many local artists; the Cathedral and the Church of Sainte

Madeleine are very fine, and the Basilica of Saint Urbain (where Princess Katherine of France was married to Henry V of England) is typical of Gothic art in Champagne. This building also contains a particularly beautiful Virgin and Child, the Madonna having the same sort of curly smile and slightly amused expression about the eyes as the famour Angel of the Annunciation on the front of Reims Cathedral, while the Baby is wholly preoccupied by an enormous bunch of grapes that He has grabbed.

From Troyes, the southern part of the Champagne region is within easy driving distance, and there are plenty of pleasant places to stay out in the country.

Travellers who are able to spend some time in Champagne should be reminded that they are also within reach of Burgundy (to the southeast) and Alsace (to the east). Paris is close and so is the Carrefour de l'Armistice in the Forest of Compiègne. To the north, the Franco-Belgian frontier and the picturesque scenery of the Ardennes are well worth exploration, perhaps from the attractive twin town of Charleville-Mézières. On the eastern edge of the region there is the great de Gaulle monument at Colombey-les-Deux-Eglises.

When to Go

French public holidays are not always the same as those in other countries, so it is worth while checking up on these before planning any short visit so as to avoid the disappointment of Champagne establishments, museums and other places of interest being closed. Don't forget, either, that although many food shops (not supermarkets) may be open on Sunday mornings – useful for buying any picnic food – Monday is generally a day when many are closed. The list of Champagne establishments open to visitors is given on page 60, but bear in mind that at weekends and especially during school and other holidays, vast crowds and parties of visitors throng the towns and queue up in many places for the organised Champagne tours. If your visit coincides with such a season, then it is a good idea to try and take part in the first tours of the morning, especially if you want to talk to the guide.

Vintage time – remember, it is later in Champagne than in other parts of France – is not always ideal for a visit. Hotel accommodation tends to be scarce and, although picking can be watched in the vineyards and the wineries will be working at full speed, few engaged in wine making will then have much time to talk.

In a good year the vineyards look magnificent in early September, when the vines are bending beneath the weight of the fruit and, day by day, the black grapes deepen in colour and the white grapes acquire an almost golden tinge. After the vintage, in late October and even early November, the vines change colour and the landscape is carpeted in gold and bright red; this is very spectacular, especially if the seasonal mists rise from the Marne and in the forests. In the spring, too, the countryside can be beautiful, with the fresh green of the vines newly in leaf. People who make a short trip to Paris at this time of year can also easily detour to Champagne – they should plan for either one whole (and long) day's excursion, or take a day and a night to see something of the region.

Planning a Visit

Enthusiasts often try to fit in too many excursions when visiting a wine region, but it is better to be selective, so that impressions subsequently remain sharp (and also so that people whose interest is not solely in the wine do not get tired and bored). Try, therefore, to vary visits to Champagne houses with trips to see something of the country, and remember also that the area is fairly extensive, so do not under-estimate the time it may take to drive around. It is possible to learn a great deal by visiting two establishments, one large and one smaller, possibly in a morning, and then following one of the recommended 'Champagne routes' out through the vineyards (see page 64) in the afternoon.

If possible, telephone or inquire first, and try to see one house in Reims (preferably with *crayères*, which are difficult to visualise without visiting them) and one in Epernay; also, you should drive over at least one of the 'routes'. It would be possible to cover all three of the main Champagne routes in a day – but this would leave no time for stopping and it is far better to allow time for halts, viewing vineyards and vines and strolling about in the villages.

If a visit can extend for more than three days (the minimum for really learning something about Champagne) or five (divided between Reims and Epernay), then time should be allocated for going down to the south of the region as well, exploring around **Sézanne, Troyes** and Bar-sur-Aube. In addition it is well worth making a detour to the Ardennes in the north if you have an extra two or three days to spare.

Seeing Cellars

Many of the Champagne cellars are well organised to receive guests and show them round, although for some it may be necessary to make a definite appointment. A number of establishments have multilingual guides so, if you are uncertain about being able to follow a commentary in French, it is a good idea to inquire in advance, so as to be sure that a guide speaking your language can be on hand.

Unless special arrangements have been made for a particular group of visitors, tours leave at regular intervals (though not usually while the establishments are shut for lunch) and take about an hour or a little more, so if you miss one time of departure, you will have to wait. However, there is usually a comfortable reception room (with a cloakroom).

Even in the height of summer, Champagne cellars are more than cool – they are cold. Guides put on top coats or thick jackets and visitors should do likewise. As some parts of the cellar may be damp and slippery underfoot, comfortable walking shoes are essential. Tourists who cannot walk far or stand much should be advised that visitors going round may have to go up and down a lot of stairs and cover quite a lot of ground; if someone cannot manage this, then it is worth remembering that the establishments of Mercier, at Epernay, and Piper Heidsieck, in Reims, can show people round in a small electric train.

It sounds unnecessary to say that people who dislike being underground should avoid such tours anyway, but sometimes visitors do not realise that the depth of the cellars is considerable, far greater than that of an ordinary wine cellar; although there is usually plenty of electric lighting, one is definitely aware of darkness. As it is not always easy for anyone suddenly upset by such surroundings to leave a tour and get back to the surface, it is better to avoid such a difficulty and remain above ground: there is usually plenty to see in the winery at ground level, and reception rooms often have interesting pictures and exhibits to look at, as well as leaflets and brochures for distribution.

Don't try and tip your guide, unless it is made obvious that this is expected. Usually, guides are employees of the firm and many are definitely in the category of 'ladies and gentlemen'. An expression of thanks is all that is required.

At the end of some tours, visitors are offered a glass of Champagne and sometimes there are special packs of wine that they can buy, although there is no obligation to do so. Remember to get a bill for any wine bought to show to the Customs on returning home. If you want to order in quantity, it is easiest to arrange to make the purchase through the representative of the house in your home country, as otherwise you will have to obtain an import licence.

If any wine appreciation group or party of serious wine lovers is fortunate enough to be invited to share the hospitality of one of the great establishments, this is naturally a memorable experience. An exquisite meal with the finest of the great wines, formally served in historic and often luxurious surroundings, will be recalled whenever a bottle bearing the name of the house is broached. As I have sometimes been asked for advice by such privileged visitors, it is perhaps helpful to state that, on these occasions (unless, of course, evening dress is specified for a very formal function, such as the reunion of one of the wine brotherhoods) guests will probably feel most at ease in the sort of clothes that they might wear at an informal party in a city – well dressed although not dressed up. Champagne is 'country', but very casual or 'holiday resort' clothes are not in keeping with the settings in which the great houses entertain. The hosts may wear 'out of town' clothes, but these tend to be smart.

It goes without saying that any appointment made to show guests round a cellar or to entertain them should be punctually kept. If not, telephone – or at least get somebody to telephone on your behalf if you are likely to be late.

Champagne Cellars that may be visited

Abel Lepître, 2 Avenue du Général-Giraud, 51100 Reims (Tel. 40.20.05)
Monday to Friday (except public holidays) by appointment only.
Closed in August.

Ayala, 2 Boulevard du Nord, 51160 Ay (Tel. 50.13.40)
Monday to Friday (except public holidays) by appointment only.

Besserat de Bellefon, Allée du Vignoble, 51100 Reims (Tel. 06.09.18)
Monday to Friday (except public holidays) 9 – 12; 2 – 5. Closed in August.

Bollinger, 16 Rue Jules-Lobet, 51160 Ay (Tel. 50.12.34)
Monday to Friday (except public holidays) by appointment only.
Closed in August.

Canard-Duchêne, Ludes, 51500 Rilly-La-Montagne (Tel. 61.10.96 Monday to Friday, and 61.11.40 Saturday, Sunday and public holidays)
Monday to Friday (except public holidays) 9-11.30; 2-4.
May 1 to September 30, also Saturday, Sunday and public holidays (visits in French only) 10-11.30; 2-5.

De Castellané, 57 Rue de Verdun, 51200 Épernay (Tel. 51.40.42)
Monday to Friday (except public holidays) by appointment only.
Closed in August.

Charles Heidsieck, 46 Rue de la Justice, 51100 Reims (Tel. 40.16.13)
Monday to Friday (except public holidays) by appointment only.

Veuve Clicquot-Ponsardin, 1 Place des Droits-de-l'Homme, 51100 Reims (Tel. 47.33.60)
Monday to Friday (except public holidays) 9 – 11.30; 2.15 – 4.30; Sunday and public holidays 2.15 – 5.30.
March 25 to October 31, also Saturday 2.15 – 5.30. February by appointment only. Closed November 1.

Coopérative Vinicole de Mancy, Mancy, 51200 Épernay (Tel. 59.71.52)
Monday to Friday (except public holidays) 9 – 11; 2 – 5. Visits in French only. Closed in August.

Deutz, 16 Rue Jeanson, 51160 Ay (Tel. 50.13.24)
Monday to Friday (except public holidays) by appointment only.

George Goulet, 4 Avenue du Général-Gouraud, 51100 Reims (Tel. 47.38.60)
Monday to Friday (except public holidays) by appointment only.

Heidsieck & Co. Monopole, 83 Rue Coquebert, 51100 Reims (Tel. 07.39.34)
Monday to Friday (except public holidays) 9 – 11; 2.30 – 4.30.
April 10 to October 31, also Saturday, Sunday and public holidays

2.30 – 4.30 by appointment only. Closed March 27 to April 9 and in August.

Henriot & Co., 3 Place des Droits-de-l'Homme, 51100 Reims (Tel. 40.38.86
Monday to Friday (except public holidays) 8 – 11.30; 2 – 5.30.

Joseph Perrier Fils & Co., 69 Avenue de Paris, 51000 Châlons-sur-Marne (Tel. 68.29.51)
Monday to Friday (except public holidays) 9 – 11; 2.30 – 5 by appointment only. Closed in August.

Krug, 5 Rue Coquebert, 51100 Reims (Tel. 47.28.15)
Monday to Friday (except public holidays) by appointment only. Closed in July.

Lanson Père et Fils, 12 Boulevard Lundy, 51100 Reims (Tel. 40.36.26)
Monday to Friday (except public holidays) by appointment only.

Veuve Laurent-Perrier, 51100 Tours-sur-Marne (Tel. 59.91.22)
Monday to Friday (except public holidays) by appointment only. Closed in August.

Louis Roederer, 21 Boulevard Lundy, 51100 Reims (Tel. 47.59.81)
Monday to Friday (except public holidays) by appointment only. Closed in July.

G.H. Martel & Co., 46 Avenue de Champagne, 51200 Épernay (Tel. 51.44.07)
Monday to Friday (except public holidays) by appointment only.

Massé Père et Fils, 48 Rue de Courlancy, 51100 Reims (Tel. 47.61.31)
Monday to Friday (except public holidays) by appointment only.

Mercier, 75 Avenue de Champagne, 51200 Épernay (Tel. 51.71.11)
January 15 to March 1, November 15 to December 23, Saturday and Sunday (except public holidays) 9 – 11; 2 – 5.
March 1 to November 15, daily 9 – 11.30; 2 – 5.30. Visit in electric train.

Moët & Chandon, 20 Avenue de Champagne, 51200 Épernay (Tel. 51.71.11)
January 2 to March 12, November 2 to December 31, Monday to Friday (except public holidays) 9 – 11.30; 2 – 5.
March 13 to October 31, Saturday, Sunday and public holidays 9 – 12; 2 – 5.30.

G.H. Mumm & Co., 34 Rue du Champ-de-Mars, 51100 Reims (Tel. 40.22.73; weekend 88.29.27)
January 1 to February 28, Monday to Friday (except public holidays) 9 – 11.15; 2 – 5.
March 1 to May 31, October 1 to October 31, daily 9 – 11.15; 2 – 5.
June 1 to September 30, daily without interruption 9 – 5.

Perrier-Jouët, 26 Avenue de Champagne, 51200 Épernay (Tel. 51.20.53)
April 9 to September 30, Monday to Friday 9 – 12; 2 – 5; Saturday, Sunday and public holidays 9 – 12; 2.30 – 5.30.

Philipponnat, 13 Rue du Pont, Mareuil-sur-Ay, 51160 Ay (Tel. 50.60.43)
Monday to Friday (except public holidays) by appointment only. Closed July 15 to August 15.

Piper-Heidsieck, 51 Boulevard Henri-Vasnier, 51100 Reims (Tel. 88.01.20)
January 1 to March 26, November 2 to December 31, Monday to Friday (except public holidays) 9 – 11.30; 2 – 5.30.
March 27 to November 1, daily 9 – 11.30; 2 – 5. Visit in electric train.

Pol Roger & Co., 1 Rue Henri-Lelarge, 51200 Épernay (Tel. 51.41.95)
Monday to Friday (except public holidays) by appointment only. Closed in August.

Pommery & Greno, 5 Place du Général-Gouraud, 51100 Reims (Tel. 47.29.51)
Monday to Friday (except public holidays) 9 – 11.15; 2 – 5.15; Saturday, Sunday and public holidays by appointment only.

Ruinart Père et Fils, 4 Rue des Crayères, 51100 Reims (Tel. 40.26.60)
Monday to Friday (except public holidays) 9 – 11; 2.30 – 4. An **appointment must be made in advance for groups over 25.**

Société de Producteurs, Mailly-Champagne, 51500 Rilly-La- Montagne (Tel. 49.41.10)
Daily 9 – 11; 2 – 6. Visits in French only.

Taittinger, 9 Place St.-Nicaise, 51100 Reims (Tel. 88.37.27)
Daily (except Christmas and New Year) 9 – 11; 2 – 5. From November to March, visits in French only.

The Champagne Routes

Before setting out on one of the routes given here, it is advisable to buy a good map of the area – Michelin Map number 56 can be used for most of your tour, but if you want to visit the south of the region you should also have number 61.

There are three main routes planned to give visitors a good general idea of the Champagne wine region. To follow any of them will enable the traveller to see a great deal of the countryside, without losing time in retracing steps; there are frequent signposts, indicating itineraries for wine-loving tourists.

The Blue Route

This starts from Reims and concentrates on the Montagne de Reims region. Leave Reims in the direction of Soissons, taking Route Nationale 31. At Thillois, turn off left to the D 27 as far as Gueux. Here keep to the left to Vrigny and Pargny-lès-Reims, where you continue on the D 26 to Sacy. This is the 'Petite Montagne', already wine country, with the well-known plantations of Jouy-lès-Reims to the left of the route and Villedommange to the right. If you stop to visit the latter, there is a fine panorama of St. Lié, just off the road, worth seeing for the view of the whole Montagne de Reims.

After Sacy, Ecueil and Chamery, the road passes through Sermiers and crosses the Route Nationale 51. This, if you follow it to the right, leads to Épernay. Just here there is also another extensive view at Mont-Chenot.

Turn left, as if going back to Reims, on the RN 51, and, almost at once, take a right turn onto the D 26 for Villers-Allerand and Rilly-la-Montagne. Continue to Chigny-les-Roses and Ludes-le-Coquet (all delightful country in which to picnic or simply to stop and look around) and, after crossing the D 9, you reach Mailly-Champagne. A short detour to the right, on the D 9, will lead to the pass of Craon de Ludes, where there is another fine vineyard view.

At Mailly, you are in particularly fine wine country, also at Verzenay and, between the two little towns, standing up in the vineyards, there is the famous windmill, the last of what were once a large number. From Verzenay you can go down into the Valley of the Vesle, to Beaumont-sur-Vesle and, turning back towards Reims, go through Sillery, one of Champagne's most famous names. But if you turn south, still on the D 26, there are fine views on the road to Verzy, a short distance away, including panoramas from the elevation of Mont Sinaï, with its observatory, a famous outpost used by General Gouraud for his offensive in World War I.

Turn on to the D 34 and then, at the small modern chapel, follow the road to the left. This leads into a forest and the extraordinary 'faux de Verzy', a type of beech (the name faux is supposed to come from the tree's Latin name, Fagus). The trees owe their odd formation to a combination of a soil in which there is a high proportion of iron and a very mild temperature – warmer than that to which this particular variety is accustomed – and they are in every sense freak growths, only reaching a moderate height and seeming to crouch on contorted trunks, with long, knotted branches, like wizened arms, reaching out seemingly to clutch at the surrounding land. To see the faux at dusk, or in the mist, is quite eerie.

After Verzy, descend to Ambonnay, then take the D 19 to the little village of Bouzy, famous for its still red wines, and procede through it to join the D 34 up to Louvois. The Château de Louvois, built by Mansart for Michel Le Tellier, Chancellor of France, subsequently belonged to the daughters of Louis XV, but most of it, except the outbuildings and gates, was destroyed in the French Revolution. The property cannot be visited, but a good view of it is obtained from the eighteenth-century wrought-iron gates, through which both the house and some of the gardens, laid out by Le Nôtre, may be glimpsed. From Louvois, you can either go down on the D 9 to Avenay-Val-d'Or, which has two interesting churches, or else return on the D 34 to the Marne at Tours-sur-Marne on the D 19. Part of the subsequent route is that of the Red Route.

The Red Route

This concentrates on the Marne Valley and can either be a convenient excursion from Épernay or can be an extension of the Blue Route, if a whole day can be devoted to exploring out in the country.

If, on leaving Épernay, you cross the Marne, take the D 1 to Ay. This is a quiet, regularly arranged wine town in which many of the great Champagne houses have headquarters, but many of the private individuals tend to hide themselves in houses built around courtyards protected by the sort of gates through which nothing can be seen. One of the more ancient houses is said to have been the winery of Henri IV.

If you go further along the Marne to the east, you will have good views of vineyards around Mareuil-sur-Ay. Otherwise, take the D 1 to Dizy and then turn right, onto the N 51, which is the main road to Reims. There are superb vineyard views from Champillon, and this is where you will find the 'Royal Champagne' establishment, a famous restaurant and hotel which has an enormous wine list of Champagnes – useful for anyone interested in trying wines that may not be seen much on export lists.

Turn off to the left onto the D 71, toward St. Imoges and, a little further on, turn left onto the N 386, past the local zoo. You will arrive at Hautvillers. Here there are also magnificent views of the vineyards and the Marne Valley. The little church contains the graves of Dom Pérignon and Dom Ruinart, marked by carefully inscribed tombstones. Notice the chandelier above the high altar – it is made from the remains of an old press. The choir stalls are also of great interest. Leading out of what is now the parish church are the remains of the once mighty Benedictine abbey; the property belongs to Moët and is not always open to the public, but for the seriously interested it is usually possible to arrange to see the cloisters with their fine modern relief of Dom Pérignon, and to enjoy the view from the terrace. Sometimes this is the scene of celebrations and fêtes in honour of Champagne.

Descend to the D 1 and turn right, along the Marne, to Cumières, another quiet little town where a good red wine is made, softer and more supple than that of Bouzy. The road follows the Marne valley through Damery, a popular place of resort of Henri IV, and Châtillon-sur-Marne, with its huge statue of Pope Urban II (who was born there), as far as Dormans, a picturesque little town on the banks of the river. In the grounds of the château is the Chapelle de la Reconnaissance, **commemorating the two Battles of the Marne.**

To extend this route, you can cross the Marne at Dormans and join to N 3 to return to Épernay.

The Green Route

This, which is limited to south of Épernay, runs through the famous Côte des Blancs, celebrated for its white wines. It is a particularly peaceful route, the shortest of the three and, if you are staying in Épernay, it can easily be accomplished, allowing for stops, in part of a morning or afternoon.

Leave Épernay by Route Nationale 51, to Pierry. Here a short détour may be made as far as St. Martin d'Ablois, through Vinay. Return and, at Moussy, just beyond Pierry, leave the main road, turn right to Chavot and descend to Monthelon, where there are good views en route. Branch off to the left to Mancy and Grauves, where there is a local saying that "The Holy Virgin of Grauves made more turns than she made miracles", because the big screw of a wine press was once transformed into a statue of the Madonna. The road (D 240) goes on to Oger, through picturesque countryside.

At Oger you join the D 10, going to Le Mesnil-sur-Oger. Here a very fine Champagne, Salon, is made. Further on is Vertus, an attractive little town with many old houses and the Church of St. Martin. This was burned in 1940, but it has been carefully restored and is worth a visit. It is attractively sited, with an adjacent small lake fed by a spring coming from St. Martin's Well, which is in the crypt of the church. Between Vertus and Bergères-lès-Vertus plantations of black grapes will again be noted, for this is the end of the long tail of the Côte des Blancs. At this point you can turn back to Oger and then branch right, keeping on the main D 10 road. This leads through Avize (one of the most famous, if not the most famous 'white' vineyard of all), and then on to Cramant. There are lovely views here over the sweeps of the vineyards and the local churches are worth visiting.

Below Cramant, sited above Chouilly, is the Château de Saran, an elegant and finely-maintained property belonging to Moët et Chandon; this house had the inspiration to make Saran into a place where visitors might be received and, in certain special instances, stay. Their considerable properties in Épernay were – and are – impressive, but these are formal settings for great occasions. Saran – which has given its name to a fine Coteaux Champenois – is a house in which people live, guests come and go and where, at impeccably presented luncheons and dinners, it is never possible to forget that this is a private dwelling,

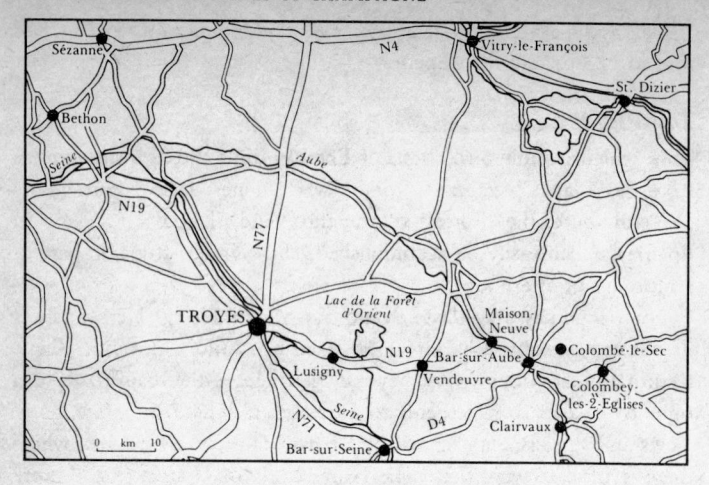

The south of the Champagne region

giving the fortunate an experience of *la vie de château* as it can be when perfected.

From Chouilly or Cramant, it is a short drive to return to Épernay.

The south of the region

Very few books on Champagne (the wine) devote much space to the south of the region. Yet anyone who can take the time should certainly try to explore something of the towns and the countryside around Sézanne, Troyes and Bar-sur-Aube. The landscape is somewhat gentler and more varied than in the north, and the works of art and museums – many of them with great relevance to the history of the wine – are undeservedly little-known. Unusual local wines will be found, and restaurateurs will demonstrate a pride in making true country specialities. Guidebooks are few, but information can be locally obtained, especially for anyone who can cope with even a little French. The inhabitants are welcoming to visitors who try to explore – and they can often provide a dry comment as to the role played by the wines made in this section of the Champagne vineyard.

For example, a great deal of wine is made in this hidden region – and a lot of it is bought by well-known establishments in Reims and Épernay. Legally, it is of course Champagne. It can be extremely useful in the great blends. But, if you taste it as a product of its region, it will display its own individuality. For example, just off the N 51 southwest of Sézanne is the village of Bethon, with, a short distance outside, the well-run co-operative of Brun de Neuville. The vineyards here are extensively planted in Chardonnay, and they enjoy the advantage of being just that extra bit south of the chillier slopes of Reims and Épernay, with some shelter from the undulations of the landscape. The wines they make, notably their Coteaux Champenois, show this extra amiability. Yet there are some among the aristocrats of the great houses who, personally, cannot accept this 'taste of Bethon' in their blends; they don't like it and its definitely individual flavour is alien to their palates. The outsider must experiment and register the particular style.

Around Bar-sur-Aube, the Champagnes are equally individual. The Confrérie Saint-Paul Saint-Vincent was founded here, in the twelfth-century cellars at Colombé-le-Sec, as recently as 1968. The Cistercians who built these cellars were part of the great organisation created at Clairvaux by Saint Bernard – but Clairvaux is today a prison, unable to be visited. The group of producers responsible for this revival of pride in the local Champagnes now possesses a *Chalet de Dégustation* (Tasting Room) just outside Bar-sur-Aube, on the RN 19, on the road to Troyes. It is open only from July until the end of September, the height of the tourist season, but seriously interested wine lovers should try to contact the President, Bernard Breuzon, at Colombé-le-Sec (Tel. 27.02.06), or the Secretary, Michel Paradis, at the Paradis establishment in the same town (Tel. 27.02.12).

Enjoying the Wine

To enjoy Champagne fully, it is important to know how to serve it correctly, which foods it complements best and, above all, which Champagnes are to your particular taste. I hope that the following notes may help to increase your enjoyment of the world's supreme sparkling wine.

Tasting Champagne

Some people say that it is difficult to taste Champagne – or, for that matter, any sparkling wine – with the same set of procedures that might be used for a still wine. They find that the *mousse* is both a distraction and a complication. Yet, as it is this *mousse* that is an integral part of Champagne when the ordinary drinker drinks it, I think it is important to consider the wine as a whole to gain an overall impression of what it is like. If, of course, you want to find out something in detail about the original wine before it was subjected to the Champagne process (and this can on certain occasions also be of great interest and importance) then let the wine go flat in the glass and taste it after a few hours.

But, in general, the stages of tasting Champagne are the same as those for a still wine: you look at the wine; you sniff it – possibly swinging it in the glass to increase the aeration; you pull it into your mouth, perhaps with a little air to sharpen the impression it first makes on the palate; then you either spit it out or swallow it and, subsequently, you register the after-taste and after-smell.

Looking at the wine

As most white wines deepen in colour as they get older, it is usual for a Champagne that has acquired more than average 'bottle age' to become more definitely golden in tone; a young Champagne will be

ENJOYING THE WINE · 71

only pale gold, sometimes even a lemon-silver-gilt colour. While the *mousse* is active, it may be somewhat tricky to determine the exact tone but, if you stare at the wine and deliberately unfocus your eyes, you will see a blur of colour that may be a more definite tone, without the distracting vivacity of the movement in the glass.

Naturally, colour varies slightly even with the non-vintage wines; even if you can compare those known to be of about the same age, it will vary, because of the variations in the proportions of grapes used and the individual variations of procedures followed by different establishments. With a vintage Champagne, the particular year may have some bearing on the colour, but this is something that has to be related both to the style of the particular house and the date when the wine was disgorged (see page 32).

A Champagne of some age tasted in the ordinary way will, of course, be on its second cork and, therefore, be showing its age more markedly than a wine only recently disgorged, offered in its home. It is often astonishing how young a wine can remain while on its first cork; I have had recently disgorged Champagnes of certain years (admittedly fine vintages) that looked, smelled and tasted truly young even when they were fifty years old! But these are always rare and great experiences.

In very general appraisal, a Champagne that has deepened in colour will be an old wine – but there are light-toned Champagnes that achieve the age of elderly wines too. Don't be misled, either, into thinking that a *blanc de blancs* will inevitably be paler in colour than a wine that includes a proportion of black grapes as well: sometimes this may be so, but sometimes it is not.

The *mousse* can be a fascinating thing to watch and can also teach much about the wine. One of the most interesting things is to observe the way in which this skein of seed-pearl-like bubbles twists within the glass, often curling to the surface to break in a circle. Just as, sometimes, a wine smells so delicious that a drinker feels almost a hesitation to drink in case the taste falls short of the fragrance, so the fortunate person eyeing a glass of Champagne may, momentarily, think it almost too enchanting to be a mere liquid to smell and drink.

A good Champagne (and any good sparkling wine as well) should be markedly 'lively': the bubbles should be tiny, they should rise fast and seem to surge towards the surface. The actual 'head' of massed bubbles that forms on the surface seldom retains its foam-like depth for more than a few seconds and it will not hold even briefly unless the glass is fairly narrow. Whereas with a vigorous young wine this head is usually deep and, momentarily, almost substantial, it tends to foam less thickly and for a shorter time as the wine ages, so that a vintage in its prime or somewhat older may have only a thin foamy cap on the surface for an instant. Yet generalisations are risky and it is my personal opinion that sometimes even an older wine will still form a fairly marked foamy head – especially if it comes out of a magnum, where its youthfulness may have been particularly well preserved.

The bubbles should continue to rise in the glass for a considerable time, unless the glass is the wrong shape, damp or affected by grease or detergent (see pages 83 to 86). For how long they should rise is impossible to say – in a young vintage and a non-vintage wine the *mousse* will be at its most lively, and the bubbles will often continue to rise for five, ten, fifteen minutes or more. Even when the wine seems to have become quite quiet, the odd minute bubble may suddenly appear and rush upwards. With an old wine, there will be less vivacity and the rush to the surface may be less turbulent, although the bubbles should still be tiny.

Sometimes, if a wine is really old, there will be very little apparent *mousse* although you may note an impression of liveliness on the palate – a suggestion of a 'prickle'. Or the wine when poured may be completely flat – this doesn't mean that it is undrinkable, but it may be a fragile antique and should be consumed soon. By the way, it is not always inevitable that a wine will be flat and old if the cork does not seem to have any 'push' behind it – sometimes one fears the worst when the cork comes out too easily and there is no suggestion of even the slightest 'burp' as it emerges, but, when the wine is poured, the *mousse* may be evident.

Smell the wine

To do this you must use a goblet or tulip-shaped glass, in which the bouquet is gathered and sent towards the nose by the incurving rim. Swing the wine around, just as you would a still wine.

The initial smell should be of fresh, clean wine with additional subtleties of fragrance presenting themselves as you sniff. Short, frequent sniffs, perhaps taking the glass away after a few sniffs and then nosing the wine afresh, will probably provide a greater number of definite impressions than a continuous inhalation.

Try to see whether the wine's smell gives an indication of its being large-scale or assertive. If it seems reserved, shake it about vigorously to release the bouquet. Is the overall smell flowery, or fruity, or herby, or leafy, or sweet or sharp? Does it seem reluctant to make itself evident to you, or does it come up immediately and make an instant effect? Has it a cool, crisp, almost tart note? Does it unfold gradually and almost luxuriantly, with a series of developing aromas, each enticing the nose to return and sniff yet again? Or do you simply not like the smell – and why don't you?

Register and, if possible, write down the impression you gain by the wine's smell before you taste it, for sometimes the smell indicates what the taste will be like and the taste thereafter complements the smell. A slightly warm, sunny smell may lead on to a wine that tastes ripe, rounded and amiable. A delicately honeyed fragrance can indicate a subtly full wine with undertones of sweetness. Sometimes, however, the taste almost contradicts the smell – as when a wine has a very crisp, piercingly fresh fragrance that then leads on to a flavour that is fruity, spread out and far more obvious than would have been expected.

If possible, try to taste several of the different Champagnes from the same establishment at a time, so as to register the house style. The vintage wine will of course possess the individuality of its year, but the vintage, non-vintage, luxury *cuvée, rosé* and *blanc de blancs* from one single house will have something in common, whether you can distinguish it most definitely on the nose or on the palate. Sometimes the common factor is most easily noted on the nose. But what you notice, immediately, is likely to be the recognisable characteristic that you will pick up quickly when you note it again.

Put your own tags on the different marques so as to help you differentiate: other peoples' tags are unlikely to be of much help, but, to give an idea of how this can work, some of my own include "Bollinger – masculine, authoritative, usually reserved with much power behind the commanding quality. Lanson – a man's Champagne, four-square, full, definite. Pommery – finely-knit, a gracious aristocrat with an unexpectedly warm smile. Roederer – nobility and sun, effortless achievement of quality. Clicquot – flowers with a touch of spice, charm backed by great firmness." But it is far better to evolve your own particular way of identifying what, to you, are the characteristics of the great Champagnes, whether you associate them with pieces of music, different flowers, racehorses, aspects of sport, literature or human beings.

Taste the wine

Draw a little wine into your mouth – only a small sip, because you want to concentrate all your powers of taste on it, rather than have it flow happily around, inundating you with general pleasure. Appraisal comes first!

As you let the wine pass your lips, draw in a little air at the same time – you needn't make more than a very discreet gurgling noise while doing so. But the way in which the wine that is being pulled into the mouth is combined with a little air will sharpen and intensify the overall impressions it makes on the palate.

Register the effect the wine has on the mouth in general – the *mousse* will make its impact quite definite. But note too the underlying flavour that backs up the tingling impression made by the sparkle – this should generally be clean and pleasant.

Then – does it seem full-bodied, or does it make a crisp, almost drying impact on the mouth? Does it unfold, like a flower opening, so that it becomes a large-scale, assertive wine? Does it give of its flavours at once – and then have nothing more to reveal? Does it snuggle up to your mouth, being enjoyable from start to finish – and in what way? Or does it puzzle and entice you, luring you on to form a quite different impression of it from the initial one? Is it a big wine or a small one, a trim one or one that seems a bit untidy at the edges? Try to form an impression of its shape in your mind – big, fat, thin, pinched, buxom, sinewy, sloppy, well-knit, clean-cut, blurred?

Do the taste sensations affect the sides of the tongue and the top and sides of the mouth as the wine demonstrates its 'bigness'? Does the wine insinuate itself, gradually, or does it announce its arrival in your mouth with a flourish? Does it start by seeming to have a single, possibly piercing style ... and then does it spread out, offering you a number of delicate but different taste sensations, each lightly jostling the other, so that you go for the second taste to try and work out which is the predominant flavour?

Don't try too hard – but do note the wine's style. Again, the initial impression you receive will probably be the one that, even after many tastings, you decide is the clearest. To go on and strain to define tastes can be a profitless task.

Tasting, done seriously, is always tiring, however enjoyable, so don't keep on for too long. But don't let your attention wander while you taste – concentrate on the wine in the glass and nothing and no one else. Even if you note only one thing it will be of lasting value to you.

After-taste and finish

When you have either swallowed the wine or – if you have a long range to tackle – you have spat out the tasting sample, then breathe out, with a definite 'huff'. You will be aware of both smells and flavours that, almost like phantoms, pass across your registers of smell and taste. These are the after-tastes and, indeed, the after-smells.

Do they evoke the initial smells and tastes first registered? Do they suggest that there is something more to both the smell and taste of the wine? (This can indicate either that there may be a future development in the wine, especially with a youngish wine, or that there is an underlying possibility of the wine evolving a different style from that immediately expected.) Do these after-tastes and smells in any way contradict the smells and tastes first noted? Sometimes a wine 'turns round in the mouth': a marked difference registered in this way can indicate that a wine is still 'finding out what it wants to be', possibly developing from what may seem to be a light, crisp, fairly delicate wine into something far more substantial, possessing a fruit and a fullness of body and substance in the after-taste that you might not have been able to perceive by any first taste impression.

The 'finish' of a wine is also indicative of its quality. Even with a sweet wine, the final impression on the palate should be one of cleanness. Of course, a sweetish wine will have a fuller and more opulent style, but it can leave the palate almost crisply, with a flick; conversely, a very dry wine can trail away in its after-taste, with a lingering, almost languorous style.

The essential is not to make up your mind in advance by what anyone may have said to you about the wine, or be influenced by what you see on the label or what you remember of previous tasting experiences. Taste only for the instant. What does the wine say to you at the second when you look at it, sniff it, pull it into your mouth, savour the 'finish'? These are the impressions to register. Don't be concerned with what is well-known, expensive, or what somebody else thinks is good – no matter who they may be. What do *you* think?

Make notes as you taste whenever possible. Even within an hour your impressions may be vaguer. If you have tasted several wines, they may each provide you with overall delight – but will this be of the slightest use to you the next time you are confronted with a wine list, or are asked to give your views about particular wines? Be as precise as you can, even if it seems affected. It will be far more useful to you, later on, if a tasting note reads "Reminds me of wet tiles recently washed with disinfectant, but with a succulent flavour that suggests flowers and trifle – ? vanilla and nutmeg – and ends with a touch of thyme and prunes." This is far more suggestive than "Very nice – should like to drink", or "Big bouquet, full-bodied". Even if you note "A bit oncoming – ? tarty – at the outset and then a touch of cough syrup", this at least shows you are truly alert to what you do and don't like. Somebody enthusiastic about the same wine might comment "Soaring bouquet – alluring first flavour, languorous follow-on". And who is to say which of you is right?

Writing tasting notes

This is as taxing and difficult as tasting itself! And no one can do it for you. Because taste is a subjective experience, only what you note down is the slightest use as a record that can remind you of what you found a wine to be like; of course, you can share your feelings that a wine is good or bad, big or small-scale, long or short and so on, but these are expressions that you can use in speech – if you are writing down impressions, then you may use your own 'shorthand' to remind you of what were your instantaneous reactions.

But do make notes while tasting. Even half an hour later your memories will have become less defined – you may have been so impressed by the last wines that you forget how critical you were of the first ones! Put down whatever comes into your mind, in as definite a way as possible. This tasting note is something for your eyes only – you can translate it into generalities in conversation, but what you write must recall your on-the-spot, at-the-moment reactions to you, for future reference. "Continental lavatories", "sucked peach stones", "cats in privet", "old velvet curtains" – all of which are terms that I use and which mean something to me – are some of my own mnemonics. Let your mind open, force your concentration to work and evolve your personal aids to remembering taste impressions. It's hard – but it is the only way in which you can tune up your tasting memory.

Always date tasting notes and, if you do not have a properly set out tasting sheet, make a precise record as to where the tasting took place and the names of the wines.

Deterrents to tasting

There are a few things that make it difficult to taste. Some – notably smoking and scent (on men as well as women) – are obvious. A cold prevents you from tasting easily, and very few people find it easy to taste after they have had a large mid-day meal. The morning, when the stomach is fairly empty and both the mind and body are fresh, is probably the ideal time. Otherwise, if you wish to prepare your palate for serious tasting, remember that violently flavoured or piquant foods can make it difficult for you, and this should also be remembered when you are choosing wines to go with a meal. Of course, few people would be silly enough to eat curry, large amounts of pickles, or anything containing a high proportion of vinegar while trying to drink a fine wine, but other things can impair the receptivity of the palate, notably eggs and chocolate. Indeed, a single chocolate makes it almost impossible for me to taste for several hours afterwards! Anything very sweet, or a piece of confectionery, will also make it quite impossible to taste for some time – even a medium dry wine will taste incredibly acid after such a thing.

People are sometimes offered crusts of dry bread or biscuits to refresh the palate at a tasting, but there is one thing that you will never accept if you are being serious about the procedure – cheese. Not for nothing do the wine trade say "we buy on apples, sell on cheese", because the alkalinity of cheese has the effect of making almost any wine taste better than it may perhaps be, whereas the acidity of an apple, or a crisp young carrot, will show up a wine quite brutally for good or bad.

Serving Champagne

It seems strange that a wine as highly regarded – and nowadays as expensive – as Champagne, should so often be incorrectly served, so that, frequently, the skilled attention of years is nullified in a few moments. Unfortunately this is so. Even in good restaurants wine butlers are either not always informed, or are not permitted by the management to serve the wine as it should be and, equally often, the ignorance of the public makes them demand unsuitable temperatures, inappropriate glasses and other totally unnecessary impedimenta, such as the 'mosser' or swizzle stick. Yet the right way to serve Champagne is simpler than the wrong way – and the results are far more gratifying.

Champagne is often served far too cold. If it – or any other wine, still or sparking – is virtually iced, then the delicate and fascinating bouquet is unable to emerge, the wine's taste is hardly apparent either and, afterwards, the drinker may find that he suffers a considerable thirst and some headache. Many people get the notion that Champagne doesn't agree with them, simply because they have had to drink a semi-frozen beverage which was not enjoyable at the time and which, because of the shock it gave to the system, had unpleasant after-effects. Over-chilling is the unscrupulous caterer's method of concealing that a wine is either out of condition or frankly inferior – so drinking it won't do much good to the consumer, although he may not complain if he can't taste it in its iced lolly form.

The correct service of Champagne is a graceful business, agreeable to the eye and, ultimately, beneficient to the palate.

The wine should be cold, because then its bouquet will rise as freshly as the bubbles, and the impact of the liquid on the mouth will be refreshing – not stunning. But the actual temperature of the bottle depends, first, on where it has been and the conditions in which it is to be drunk: obviously a wine that comes from a cool, dampish cellar, that is probably about 10°–12° C, will require little additional chilling; indeed, on a cool day I personally would find it quite cool enough to enjoy. But a bottle kept in 'living' conditions may be warmer than this and, therefore, require some chilling. If the temperature in the room where it is to be drunk is high, and especially if the weather is stuffy, drinkers may prefer the wine to be more definitely cold: this certainly applies if you are drinking out of doors in the sunshine.

In addition, a wine with more sweetness than usual will benefit by being slightly – only slightly – colder than a very dry wine. Some people may also find, with a little experience, that they prefer certain marques of Champagne to be cooler than others – wines with a pronounced fruitiness, for example, can have this, as it were, 'polished up' by a little extra chilling, whereas a delicate wine, such as certain *blancs de blancs*, will hardly need to be brought below what may be assumed to be cellar temperature. The same applies to vintage wines: the more fragile old ones should not be chilled to the same extent as those that are young and vigorous.

Some people prefer a pink Champagne to be less cool than an ordinary non-vintage – it is, after all, half-way to being a red wine. But all this is a matter of personal preference and must be related also to when and where the wine is to be drunk – merely clinging to absolutes as regards temperatures, such as putting a type of thermometer round the bottle or into the wine is affectation: the wine goes into the mouths and bodies of human beings and should please them as it does so, regardless of the reading on some gadget. Put your hand on the bottle and you will soon get to know whether the wine inside it is likely to be satisfactorily chilled in relation to your own body temperature. (Of course, if you are in a feverish condition, your judgment will not be reliable – but then you will anyway be unlikely to be drinking fine wine!)

The swiftest way to chill any wine is in a bucket of ice and water – not ice alone, which will merely chill patches of the bottle. The level of ice and water should come up to the level of the wine in the bottle, forming a jacket that will bring down the temperature without shocking the wine. People often talk about 'bruising the gin' when making a cocktail, but they will subject fine wine to far greater shocks by putting bottles in the freezer. In general, it will take about an hour and a half or more (up to 2½ hours) to chill a wine in an ordinary domestic refrigerator, but a mere 12 to 15 minutes to achieve the same result in an ice bucket.

If, for some reason, you are opening a bottle on a hot day and are in a hurry, put the glasses in the refrigerator (never the freezer, or they may break when taken out), so that the first pourings of the wine go into a cold receptacle. Don't keep Champagne in the refrigerator – not only may it get far too cold, but it will develop a dreary, flat, lifeless character and never quite recover. And of course, if you have *had* to put bottles in the freezer in an emergency, don't forget to take them all out before they freeze – frozen wine is not only undrinkable but, even when thawed, never quite right; and there is always the danger of the bottles exploding in the freezer as the frozen liquid expands.

Opening the bottle

Never do this without having a cloth in which you can hold it. First, the cloth serves to wipe the bottle dry of any water or condensation, then it protects your hand while you are undoing the muzzle and extracting the cork – bottles seldom do split nowadays, but it is a risk not worth taking – and it will catch and blot any wine that foams up as soon as the cork comes out.

Bear in mind that the pressure inside the bottle will be increased if you shake the bottle – or if it has been bounced around in a shopping basket or in the boot of a car. Also remember that, if a bottle has been standing up for some time, the cork may have become dry and hard, which will often make it more difficult to ease out.

From the time you start to open a bottle of Champagne, never leave go of it and never release the hold of your hand on the top of the cork. You cannot know, as you begin to undo the muzzle, whether the cork is likely to rush out or whether it may take some easing, but don't forget that the pressure behind it is as great as that in the huge tyre of a London bus – and, therefore, you are holding something that, without control, is potentially likely to cause damage or injury as it emerges unless you keep at least your thumb or the palm of your hand over the mushroom. Naturally, it depends on whether you are right- or left-handed as to which way round you open the bottle, but sometimes people who are, ordinarily, right-handed, find that their left hand and arm seem to be stronger – I do myself.

Have a glass within easy reach and hold the bottle, in the cloth, in one hand. Tilt it at an angle of about 45° away from you, taking care that it does not point at anything breakable or at any person. This tilting, which moves the air in the bottle away from the cork, slightly lessens the pressure behind this. With the thumb of the same hand that holds the bottle being firm on top of the mushroom of the cork, use the other hand to pull off the top of the foil capsule (nowadays some of these capsules are perforated, so as to tear more easily): the wire muzzle is then exposed. Untwist the loop of this. Generally, this means turning it anti-clockwise, but some wines do have muzzles wound the other way, so have a look before you begin to twist. If the wire breaks off, then you must either manage to lever the whole muzzle upwards off the cork or get some nippers to cut the wire – but at no time release your hold on the mushroom.

Slip the wire right off the mushroom, keeping your hand over this for all but the second when you discard the muzzle. This is the moment when you may already feel the cork begin to rise under your hand – keep a firm grasp on it and, if possible, do this with a corner of the napkin between your hand and the cork. None of this is as complicated as it sounds, and it takes very little time.

If the cork does not move then, with the hand holding the bottle, give the bottle a turn, while retaining a steady grasp on the cork with the other hand. *Turn the bottle, not the cork.* If you try to turn the cork, it is unlikely that you will shift one that is sticking tightly, and you are likely to break off the top of the mushroom (see page 82 for how to deal with this).

As you turn the bottle you will feel the cork begin to rise, and you will find that the cork emerges (and is caught by you) with a fat, satisfied, discreet noise, instead of an explosion. The wine will rush up the bottle and you can direct it into the glass waiting nearby. In the ordinary way, nobody wants to waste even a mouthful of anything as precious as Champagne, and the explosion of a flying cork can be dangerous. True, honour is done to special visitors to Champagne houses by a *'feu de joie'* – when they walk between rows of peaked-capped, overalled cellarmen, who deliberately 'pop' bottles of Champagne to salute them – but such experienced persons as cellarmen have mighty strength in their hands to control the exact emergence of the cork, and their houses can afford to be prodigal with the foaming wine.

Because the *mousse* will be very lively immediately after the bottle is opened, it tends to rise high in the glass, so that only a small quantity of actual wine can be poured. Be prepared for this, as otherwise you will pour too much and the glass will overflow. Because the wine rises in the neck of the bottle, it can overflow unless you pour the helpings out with fair speed but, if you have only a couple of glasses to serve and wish to check any likelihood of the *mousse* coming out of the lip of the bottle and down the side, then put the palm of one hand over the lip of the bottle for a few seconds: this will check the *mousse*, because the slight grease that is on the skin of the hand acts like the greased collar to a soufflé dish – the foam can't climb up the slippery surface. Of course, this is not the sort of action one would expect to be taken by a *sommelier* in a luxury restaurant, and if you do it at home, in front of people, it might be a good idea to shield the action of your hand with the ever-present napkin.

If the cork sticks

Suppose the cork simply will not yield to the usual method of easing it out? There are Champagne nippers, which grip the mushroom and can be used to lever it upwards – although sometimes they do begin to break it off. There is also a very ingenious Italian device by which a clamp is attached to the flange under the bottle lip, a pair of claws take hold of the cork and, by the action of a reversed screw, as the screw is turned the claws pull the cork upwards: because the whole device is attached to the bottle by the clamp, the cork cannot fly out. However, it is usually possible to start a cork moving by gradually easing it upwards by the pressure of the thumbs – but don't forget to keep your fingers over the top of the cork while you do this. Once the cork starts to shift, extract it by turning the bottle in the way previously described.

If, however, you get into a situation where the cork appears to be immoveable and virtually part of the bottle, there is a very simple way to get it out. Don't try wedging it in window-frames or door-jambs – you may splinter the paint, crack the bottle and waste a lot of wine. Keep hold of the cork all the time and, having put a glass ready nearby, hold the neck of the bottle under a stream of hot water for a few seconds. The heat of the water will increase the pressure slightly inside the bottle, so that this will push out the cork.

If you have broken off the mushroom top of the cork, the remainder of it may also be extracted by holding the bottle neck under the hot tap for a few moments – but don't forget to have your hand ready to receive the cork as it comes out. The hot water treatment, taught me by a great head cellarman, is one that I have never known to fail. Suppose, however, that you do not want to carry the bottle from the room in which you are going to drink the Champagne – maybe the hot tap is some distance away? Or suppose you are on a picnic? Keep one hand over the top of the broken cork – always. First, trim off any jagged bits of cork with a sharp blade. Then, with a corkscrew, gradually pierce the remaining section of cork – gradually, because there will still be pressure behind it and this is what must now be gently released. The cork, being in layers, will be somewhat tough, so go slowly and firmly. As the corkscrew goes through and eventually pierces the cork, you will hear a 'hiss' as the gas inside comes out – hang on to the corkscrew and cork, in case it still manages to blow both away from the bottle. But, when the immediate pressure has been eased, you can – still holding on to the cork – use the corkscrew to pull the remainder of it as you would for a still wine.

And suppose you haven't got a corkscrew? Or a hot tap? Or simply haven't got time to prise up the cork? Shake the bottle – vigorously – after having removed the muzzle, and be extremely careful not to point the bottle at anyone or anything. The agitation, which will increase the wine's vivacity, will usually push the cork out. This is why victors in sporting events are often seen holding bottles of Champagne high above their heads and waving them furiously. Purists recurrently write deploring the 'casual' way in which the celebration wine is treated on such occasions – they forget that, both for the victor's deserved bumper and for the cameramen, that cork has got to come out fast! "In victory you deserve it – in defeat you need it".

Glasses

Just as it seems extraordinary that so many people should abuse a wine as fine as Champagne by the way they serve it, so it is past understanding why so often the glasses used for one of the great wines of the world are hideous, unsuitable – and definitely inimical to the wine.

In numerous old pictures, the glass shown from which people are drinking the sparkling wine is the elongated flûte, which is tall, narrow and in shape like an isosceles triangle, standing on its apex. Sometimes the base of the bowl of this glass is rounded, sometimes it goes down to a definite point. The reason why this is so suited to the consumption of Champagne is that the wine is able to enjoy maximum contact with the glass and does not spread out – so it retains its vicacity, the wonderful sparkle and spiral of bubbles, for as long as possible.

There are various other types of glass shape in use for Champagne, but all of them promote the sparkle. Some, old-fashioned ones, are like deep cups; they have hollow stems, so that the wine rises from the very foot of the glass through this narrow channel – and delightful it looks, although such glasses are awkward to clean and dry. Others, of tulip shape, often have pointed bases to the bowls and sometimes these are very elongated. There is a beautiful glass made in the famous Baccarat factory, the bowl of which is shaped like a tulip of crystal, and it is so fine that it will give slightly to the gentle pressure of the hand and, when the wine is poured into the tulip bowl, the tall stem can be felt to sway slightly with the weight. Some glasses are more like very narrow tumblers on a foot or with a stem, the bowls having sides that are almost parallel; antique glasses like this are often finely engraved. There is a Sèvres porcelain *coupe*, poised on a crystal stem and supported in a frame of silver and gilt rams' heads, which was one of a set of four made for the Queen's Dairy Temple at the Château de Rambouillet – the deep cups, with their pointed base, are said to have been moulded from the breasts of Marie Antoinette. Madame Claude Taittinger sometimes uses a set of glasses originally commissioned by the family from Lalique, the exquisite glassworks often associated with a pearly blue tint and fine engraving; hers, however, are clear, their large bowls like slightly opened tulips. In the base of each bowl is a faint engraving – like an inspired finger-tracing – depicting the slanting smile on the face of the enigmatically amused angel on the front of Reims Cathedral; the face is delicately traced up the sides of the glass and is an enchanting background for the effervescence. The great artist in glass, René Lalique, was actually born in Aÿ. And there are the onion-shaped 'Paris' goblets, found in most public houses, which are equally pleasant in form.

Every single one of these glasses – goblets, trumpet-shaped containers and, even, elongated tumblers (I have some myself, in cut crystal, made by Rosenthal and intended for the elegant service of ale or beer) – all these shapes will serve the wine to advantage. What will *not* do is the horrible so-called 'Champagne' glass that appears to have become fashionable in Britain during the last century: a shallow saucer, the bowl being out of proportion to the stem and foot and therefore top-heavy, holding a mean measure, with the sides of the bowl sloping outwards. This glass not only holds very little, but, by allowing the wine to spread out and become exposed to the air, it 'flattens' it quickly; the out-curving bowl makes it quite impossible for the drinker to smell the wine at all – one cannot swing it round without it splashing over the side – and, as the wine reaches the mouth in an uncontrolled wave against the lips, the consumer receives it in a splash, without any chance to savour and appreciate its qualities.

Unfortunately, this horrible 'saucer' glass, which I think must have been evolved so that parsimonious Victorians could eke a dozen or more helpings from a bottle, is repeatedly manufactured by British glassworks who should know better (their obsession with cutting and engraving the bowls of glasses means that nothing of this kind is suitable for the service of fine wine) and glass departments and shops continue to sell 'Champagne' glasses as part of their 'suites' of glass, thereby persuading the customer to spend money that would be better allocated to a few decent bottles of wine, even if these had to be drunk from a Paris goblet bought in a chain store. If you have saucer glasses and want to use them, keep them for the sparkling perry with which they have been associated in advertising campaigns, or fill them with ice-cream or custards. They are unfit for any wine that is fit to drink.

Sometimes people find it pleasant to drink Champagne from silver tankards or goblets. Indeed, this is often the way Black Velvet (see page 92) is served. There are two possible disadvantages: unless the silver is really well cleaned, you will get the taste of polish in your mouth, and of course you will not see the beautiful colour and *mousse* of the wine. Personally, I don't like to feel the metal between my lips, any more than I like to feel a very thick piece of glass there, no matter how beautifully cut or historic it may be. The glass is to set off the wine, not to obtrude itself. But this is a matter of personal taste. However, before you decide that I am being somewhat 'precious', make the experiment of drinking exactly the same wine from a glass that is the right shape – and from one that isn't. If possible, continue the comparison by trying the same Champagne from an ordinary cheap glass, albeit of satisfactory shape, and from a thin crystal tulip or *flûte*. You will be astonished at how much better the wine from the fine glass will taste.

But unfortunately there are various hazards to do with glasses, even if these seem to be satisfactory. Of course, a glass should be absolutely clean, clear and without smears. But it can, even so, retain undesirable smells and taints which sometimes cause drinkers to reject a wine which may be perfectly all right.

Don't store glasses bowl downwards. Stale air inside them can linger and affect the wine when they are brought into use; this is even more of a risk if they stand on anything plastic, or on a painted or polished surface, which will give them a definite smell. Keep them upright, with a piece of paper or clean napkin over the top to keep out the dust if they are not often in use. Always smell a glass before you use it and, if it does seem a bit stale and you haven't the time to wash and dry it, swing it through the air vigorously.

The washing and drying of glasses is of real importance, and even more so for those used for Champagne. A glass that is in any way greasy or that retains traces of detergent, either from being insufficiently rinsed or from being polished with a dirty cloth or one that itself retains smells from being used to dry dishes, or else a cloth that hasn't been properly rinsed free of detergent, will not only make the Champagne stink and flatten it, often completely, but it can turn the wine a horrible coarse salmon pink. Personally, I never use anything but hot water to clean glasses, and never use either soap or detergent – just near-boiling water – to clean the cloths for drying them.

If you drink Champagne in a restaurant, pay particular attention to the glasses before the wine is poured – they may have emerged immaculate from a washing machine, but then have been left standing upside down on a table or tablecloth that has a distinct smell, or else have received a final polish with a cloth that has been used for many other purposes – and that stinks.

Gadgets

There are only two gadgets that are worth noting in this context. The first is the useful device whereby an unfinished bottle can be stoppered so that the wine retains its sparkle. There are two types, one that simply clips down over the bottle lip and another that works by means of the stopper itself expanding to fill the bottle's neck when a lever is pulled down to attach it to the side. Both are wholly satisfactory, but the lever type, which is not seen as often as the other, has the advantage that it will stopper a magnum as well as a bottle. The clip type will of course stopper a half bottle, but it won't fit over the opening of a magnum. If you are administering small helpings of Champagne to a convalescent – and it is the finest tonic in the world – then use a bottle or a half size and stopper it; quarter bottles, the contents of which will have been decanted from full-size bottles (see page 46) are really only useful on aeroplanes. Stoppered bottles can be kept in the least cool part of a refrigerator or, preferably, in a bucket of cold water; the wine will remain in good condition for a couple of days if it is in a cool place. A small helping will not only encourage the appetite of an invalid when taken as an apéritif, but also the sparkle, which is deliciously refreshing in the mouth, accelerates the wine's stimulating action more than any still wine.

The other gadget, however, is wholly detestable and utterly to be condemned. It is the fancy swizzle stick or 'mosser', often gilt or gold, sometimes presented to drinkers in nightclubs or restaurants that ought to know better, when it appears as a wooden stick with a ridged knob on the end. The purpose of this thing is to whisk the Champagne and thereby take the sparkle out of it – for which the drinker is paying and which has taken years to cultivate. If for any reason people find that a sparkling wine does not suit their constitution or if they simply want something still, then why do they not order such a wine – and refrain from abusing Champagne? Or, with the several excellent *crémant* Champagnes now available, why don't they select a wine with slightly less *mousse*?

Champagne – With What?

Few would dispute the statement that a dry or a good non-vintage

Champagne is the perfect apéritif, creating a liveliness of spirit and stimulating the taste-buds – a summons to the appreciation of fine food. But – is it always so? Can it really be served all through a meal, and with what?

One is often informed that Champagne – as a sparkling wine—is for any-time drinking, that it is suitable for any hour of the night or day and able to go right through the courses of any meal. Yet ... can it really be the perfect accompaniment to smoked salmon or raw ham and melon, to jugged hare or steak and kidney pudding, or to *profiterolles au chocolat* or Christmas pudding?

As a lover of the wines of Champagne, I venture to suggest that, given the opportunity to select from their great variety, there are wines for many occasions and dishes – yet that there are also some occasions and dishes that do not partner Champagne so that its qualities can be appreciated.

People often do not realise that Champagne is not only a sparkling wine but one fairly high in alcohol; therefore, the impact made by the *mousse* upon the palate is, very slightly later, reinforced by the power behind the bubbles. Still or sparkling, wine from Champagne also has considerable weight, in the sense of the wine having a definite substance and making a lasting impression. Therefore, it makes an immediate effect and quickly creates a party or a special occasion but, because of its importance, its weight, its alcoholic content and the way in which the *mousse* in the sparkling wine makes such a definite impression on the palate, any foods served with this wine – and certainly any wines served immediately after it – must be of equal quality, importance and weight.

You cannot, for example, serve a very delicate still table wine for the first course of a meal when you have offered a fully sparkling Champagne as the apéritif. It simply cannot make any impression on a palate already impressed and tuned up by the bubbles. A wine to follow the supreme sparkler must be a big one, of equal quality – and this, in my view, is where the Coteaux Champenois wines are most useful, because they do have the weight and a certain forcefulness that enables them to stand the immediate comparison, whereas, to quote one of the greatest of English wine merchants, the late Ronald Avery, "Champagne will kill the finest white Burgundy if you serve the one immediately after the other". (And he was an authority on white Burgundy.) So, if you start with Champagne but cannot serve one of the region's wines to follow, or something else of equal weight, or if you do not wish to continue by serving a slightly more 'important' Champagne of the sparkling sort, then I suggest that the first course of the meal is a 'blotting paper' one: consommé, a creamy vegetable soup, or something such as avocado vinaigrette, herring in sour cream with onions and apples, or any salad type of dish with which one would not anyway plan to serve wine.

With many fish dishes and poultry, Champagne – either fully *mousseux* or *crémant* – is excellent, because its freshness can cut the unctuousness of any eggy, buttery or creamy sauce and balance the fatness of fish such as turbot, halibut and salmon, or the succulence of a *poulet de Bresse* (chicken roasted with butter), *faisan normande* (pheasant with cream, calvados and apples), chicken Kiev (the breasts of chicken stuffed with butter and then fried, so that they literally burst with the fat when pierced with a fork), or similar fish or poultry recipes. The same applies to any chicken recipe with a creamy sauce, or to chicken chaudfroid or, of course, to duck – with this fatty bird Champagne is excellent – and succulent small game birds, from the pigeon to the partridge. "We meet with Champagne and a chicken at last!" is Lady Mary Wortley Montagu's suggested reconciliation snack as early as the eighteenth century.

Champagne is often served with a supper dish and also as a buffet wine. I don't recommend a fine version if the supper is something piquant, or if the buffet includes the type of salad that is too 'British' by being over-doused with vinegar. However, with many cold cuts – fish or poultry with a mayonnaise made with lemon and, perhaps, given extra lightness with an added egg white, or a French dressing in the proportions of five or six of oil to one of wine vinegar – Champagne can hold its own. It will enhance even modest fare, such as quiches, chicken pie, cold potato omelette (*tortilla*), kedgeree, pasta with cream and mushrooms, and salads that include rice or potatoes – for this wine really is the charmer that can make veal and ham pie or corned beef with a baked potato into a memorable '*petit souper*'.

With such cold cuts as may include the pâtés of the Champagne region or anything similar, and fish, poultry or game, it is also excellent for cutting their richness. But with *andouillettes* or hot dishes of this type, I prefer the still wines and, usually, the red ones; they are robust and not easily swamped. For a rich fish mousse, perhaps a Coteaux Champenois *blanc* is the best choice. The complexity of some dishes seems to require a less complex, more straightforward drink and this applies, in my opinion, to dishes of certain game birds or to very delicate fish such as trout – in which the shades of flavour are in the food even when it is very simply cooked (which it should be, if it is of prime quality); so in these instances the wine, I think, ought to take a slightly more subdued place, giving pleasure without asserting itself.

Can Champagne be served with red meat? Yes – if you can find the right Champagne! I recall a wonderful luncheon to celebrate an important anniversary of Veuve Clicquot, when we drank an old pink Champagne with prime roast beef and Yorkshire pudding – the subtle fruitiness of the wine was perfect with the meat. But it *was* a twenty-year-old vintage of a great year, and it had been disgorged in Reims that morning and flown over for the occasion. Usually, in my view, red meat and strong game dishes are best accompanied by red wines. Fortunately, there are now those of the Coteaux Champenois for these occasions. But, if you possess old vintage Champagnes, it may be worth trying them against a game dish such as partridge or pheasant; gentle and fruity, they may be perfect, although I'd have something red in reserve.

With sweet dishes, the softer, even definitely sweet Champagnes are the best accompaniment – if you have been drinking wines of moderate dryness with the preceding dishes, the service of a bone dry Champagne after them will be a mistake; the wine will taste shrill, hard, ungracious. This is the time to pour a gently maturing vintage wine or – so sadly neglected in the United Kingdom – a definitely sweet Champagne. If the sweet course is heavily flavoured with chocolate or liqueurs, then any wine will certainly be wasted, but with a fruit tart or pastry, or one of the delectable meringued recipes, a 'bosomy' Champagne or perhaps one of the fruitier *rosés* is gorgeous. Indeed, the hostess who can offer fine dessert fruit such as peaches, nectarines, apricots or just prime grapes need have no other wine. It is even possible, with the sympathy of the company, to skip the sweet and offer a wonderful 'rich' or '*demi-sec*', for slow appraisal before the coffee. These beautiful wines merit more attention – and, it should be noted, they can also be wonderful apéritifs in certain contexts: the late Philip Harben would give dinner guests in winter the choice of 'dry or sweet' in Champagne – depending on whether they felt tired and wanted the cosiness of the gentler wine, or a more vivacious drink. I myself offered the Roederer Rich as an alternative to the non-vintage at a luncheon organised at the City of London's Guildhall for food and drink journalists on a frosty morning. More than half of them opted for the 'Rich' – and they had reason for so doing! But of course immediately after such an apéritif you should not serve any very dry still wine, as it will taste weak and sour.

Then there are the foods with which Champagne in its sparkling form is traditionally and rightly associated: oysters and caviare. It is admirable with both – but go easy on any squeezes of lemon or twists of the peppermill. I am not sure about Champagne with smoked fish, even smoked salmon: all right perhaps if you have previously been drinking Champagne, but the flavour of the fish does tend to blot out any impression that the wine can make. The same applies to smoked trout and smoked eel and to any smoked meats such as ham, beef, turkey or chicken.

If you have a choice from among the wines of Champagne, how should they be selected for any occasion or entertainment? Naturally, for the always and any-time celebration or consolation, or simply to dress up lightly flavoured humble fare, it is a non-vintage that comes to the rescue.

If you stay with Champagne for a meal prefaced by the non-vintage as apéritif, then I think that, ideally, you must progress to a slightly better wine; a Coteaux Champenois, either red or white, will break the wines up. However, if more sparkling wine is to be served, then it should really be a vintage and, if there is to be a third wine, then that should be a luxury *cuvée* or an older and finer vintage – for one must always end on a high note.

The great ladies of Champagne who entertain, however, are usually definite that a sparkling wine all through a meal of several courses can tax the digestion and overwhelm the food. They generally break the sequence with at least one still wine and, possibly, introduce a classic French red from Bordeaux or Burgundy with the cheese, which of course in France is served before anything sweet. This seems ideal to me. It is then possible to finish the meal with one superb sparkling wine or, later, the brandy of the region.

Champagne as an 'occasional' wine

It is obvious that any mixed drink with Champagne as an ingredient will utilise only the non-vintage. People who marry off their daughters and insist on vintage or even a luxury *cuvée* for the occasion are being silly – a wedding is a time for quaffing, not for considering. If you want to offer something extra-special at the end of a party of any kind, then the single glass of a great wine is of course a compliment – if you think that the guests are in a condition to appreciate it by then. Personally, I think that the greatest Champagnes so deserve considered appraisal that I serve them only when it is possible to drink them slowly, with a few friends whom I wish to honour – to whom I wish to reveal the glories of this wine at its finest. Such Champagnes are not general party wines.

If you are drinking Champagne in the morning, then a light, zingy wine is probably pleasantest – a reliable B.O.B. perhaps, or a *blanc de blancs*, or even a young vintage if you can be a little extravagant. Later in the day, you may feel that a fruitier, gentler type of wine such as a full bodied non-vintage, or a *crémant*, will be the best preface to a leisurely dinner. If you have been out and return to have a light snack, then a wine that will double as apéritif and go on with the food is required – perhaps a *rosé*, or a vintage that has acquired a gracious charm. Or, for the very special hour when you relax with sympathetic friends and simply want to share a beautiful drink that will discreetly enhance the mood of the company, a luxury *cuvée* will do honour to the occasion.

The still wines are excellent with many dishes that, otherwise, pose problems: Coteaux Champenois as a white wine is fine with fat fish, certain poultry or light meat recipes and, in my view, even with that difficult meat, ham – preferably if this has been cooked in Champagne or has the wine in the sauce. It is a sufficiently robust wine to stand up to fat, rich sauces or such garnishes as truffles, diced ham or fatty fungi. The red wines are also assertive – clean-cut, good for balancing enriched sauces and fatty meats or, by contrast, providing a soaringly fresh, fruity flavour against a food that might otherwise risk seeming weakly agreeable – certain chicken dishes, pork and veal.

There is virtually an appropriate Champagne for any occasion, formal or casual, but this must not be taken to mean that any Champagne will do for all occasions. The more one learns about this fascinating wine, the more shades of style become apparent and the more interesting it is to attempt to make exactly the right choice for any occasion when you are planning to open a bottle. The fortunate will have a range of wines from which to choose, but the intelligent will use their knowledge and experience so that, even if they have to buy one bottle in a hurry from a supermarket, or order from a wine list, they will be able to pick one that will give them especial pleasure, which is not always directly related to the cost.

Champagne Drinks

Many are firm in the opinion that the world's supreme sparkling wine cannot be drunk mixed with others – it must be appreciated by itself. But, just as there are occasions when one wants to read a 'good bad book', eat beans on toast, or relax to music that deserves the adjectives 'kitsch' and 'schmaltz', or simply have a change of drink that *is* a change – even if it afterwards sends one back to the original – so there are times when certain drinks made with Champagne can be light-hearted pleasures.

There are several such drinks:

Black Velvet is probably the simplest – half and half Champagne (non-vintage, of course) and stout, preferably Guinness. This is a fat, nourishing type of beverage and, for those who are wanting a drink to accompany a meal of, say, a plate of oysters, half a lobster, potted crab or humbler shellfish or crustacea, it is good value. Black Velvet was very popular in oyster bars and shellfish restaurants with counter service when Champagne was less expensive than it is today. It was traditionally associated with late Victorian and Edwardian nightlife – the Empire Promenade, 'stage-door Johnnies' and the belief that oysters were an aphrodisiac – as well as lingering even until today as a race course refresher.

King Pimm's or **Royal** is another drink that, when people are feeling opulent, is an indulgence: Pimm's Cup (No.1, the original, with a gin base) diluted with Champagne instead of the usual fizzy lemonade (in the U.S.A. they add soda with added citric acid, as fizzy lemonade is unknown). This is an insidiously 'moreish' drink – I have tried it at a party when certain jugs had the addition of Champagne and others not. Nobody noticed the difference ... except that those of us who had the 'King' began to realise that we were more 'beautiful people' than anyone else. I would say that to use Champagne in this way really is a waste of a great wine – but it can be beautifully wasted.

Buck's Fizz is a delicious drink. It was invented at Buck's Club in Mayfair in 1921 by the then barman, Pat McGarry, whose son still makes it – one-third orange juice, two-thirds Champagne (the original was non-vintage Bollinger) and a teaspoonful of grenadine. There are other versions, and other sparkling wines are used to make them.

The only opinion I hold about this, which is a gorgeous mid-morning luxury in winter or summer, is that the orange juice must be both freshly squeezed and chilled. A group of world-experienced drinkers helped me conduct tastings to establish the affirmation that nothing out of a bottle, freezer pack, carton, container saying "only fresh orange juice", or even freshly-squeezed orange juice that has remained several hours in the refrigerator, will do. None will. The oranges should be lightly chilled and then squeezed. And, ideally, they should not be too sweet – it is the crisp acidity of the fruit, without its having the tang removed from it by filtration of the 'bits' that, combined with the wine, makes this nectar. It is up to the individual as to whether the proportions are one-third orange and two-thirds wine, or half and half. Personally, I skip the grenadine and use two-thirds wine to one-third orange juice.

French 75 is a bizarre drink: 2 fluid oz. gin, a teaspoonful of sugar and the juice of half a lemon, topped up with chilled Champagne in a big glass. I find this unsatisfactory, not simply because it mixes grape (the wine) and grain (the gin), but because I don't think the lemon combines with the wine, especially with the sugar – one seems to cancel out the other. But you can experiment.

A **Champagne Cocktail**, however, can be a good drink of its kind. It is costly to order in a bar, but not very expensive if you want to make it at home. One good Champagne Cocktail can be a treat to offer a host before one is taken out to dinner.

There are several versions of how it should be made but, having experimented, the version I like best and which has been approved by many of the wine trade, is as follows: in a large glass or goblet (double the size you would use for an ordinary drink) put a lump of sugar which has been rubbed over the skin of an orange. On this sugar lump drop 2 or 3 drops of Angostura Bitters. Over it, pour a teaspoonful of brandy (ideally Cognac or Armagnac) and also a teaspoonful of an orange-based liqueur, such as Curaçao, Cointreau, or else a peach or apricot brandy. Personally, I use rather more spirit, in the proportions of two-thirds brandy (a dessertspoon) to one-third (a large teaspoon) of liqueur. Allow the sugar to dissolve in the spirit for at least an hour or more – this is the secret of this version. When ready to serve, top up the glass with a chilled non-vintage Champagne. The dissolving of the sugar in the spirit beforehand makes an astonishing difference to the drink – a mixture prepared in minutes never tastes as good. So – use a big glass and give a single good drink.

If a garnish is thought appropriate, then the glasses can be 'frosted' by rubbing the rims with a cut segment of orange and then dipping them in caster sugar, twisting a cut segment of orange over the finished drink (it is important to squeeze the *skin* of the orange, so as to release the oils in it) and hanging a chunk of orange on the edge of the glass.

There are many variations on this drink. Because it is 'grape and grape' it may be served before a meal that is to be accompanied by fine wines. (But it should be remembered that Champagne can overpower many of even the finest of these). The pre-Revolution Russian nobility used to make a mixture of yellow Chartreuse topped with Champagne – very strong and, if one can rely on recollections of such a drink, somewhat coarsely stunning. The Paris Ritz top up a measure of Poire Williams with Champagne, and there is also 'Champagne cassis' – blackcurrant liqueur similarly topped up. (I think this is too sweet, unless the Champagne is exceptionally dry).

Some years ago a London restaurant used to make a delightful version by putting a measure of Chambéryzette (Chambéry vermouth flavoured with alpine strawberries) into the glass before the Champagne, and I have also been given others with a base of kirsch or mirabelle – the strength of the colourless liqueur gives the drink a great 'kick', but I don't think these fruits combine as well as the orange ones with the wine. The chic Jockey Club in Paris is said to omit the brandy, but to garnish the glass with a slice of pineapple plus a twist of zest of a fresh lime, and then to pour a measure of Cointreau (which of course is based on orange) on the top of the drink. Frankly, it sounds unbalanced to me – I would think that the Cointreau (most admirable of liqueurs) would nullify the flavour of whatever wine was first in the glass. A fearful thing called the Shanghai Cocktail uses kümmel in conjunction with brandy, advocates rubbing the glass with lime or lemon zest and floating a rose on the drink. I may be prejudiced but, even without tasting it, the ingredients are fighting on my taste-buds.

There are occasions when it is permissible to touch up even the charms of Champagne. But, when a good bottle results in a whirl of furiously-rising seed pearls of harvest-moon gold bubbles from the point of a finely proportioned glass . . . then the nose appreciates the soaring fragrance, the palate the delectable, alluring charm and the mind the fascination that makes one take the second mouthful to try to determine its exact nature . . . lovers of Champagne may stray but, always and ever, they will return to love their love, like truth, as a naked lady, because she is so simply and infinitely beautiful.

Champagne Gastronomy

Champagne can give a misleading impression of its regional gastronomy to any traveller who eats only in luxury hotels and restaurants. In such places, the numerous dishes "au Champagne" are, naturally, aimed at appealing to the palates of the well-to-do or to anyone giving a party on a special occasion. The use of the local wine in the sauce for a dish, or for poaching fish, meat, poultry or fruit is usual in any wine region and, in Champagne, the wine used will generally be the still type or, for certain stews, the red wine. But, of course, the sprinkling of the word "Champagne" over the menu gives an impression of outstanding luxury – and may likewise imply considerable expense.

It is, therefore, worth trying to eat off the beaten track, because Champagne's proximity to Paris and its situation as a convenient stopping place for tourists coming up from Spain and making for the north, or crossing from the Channel ports to the east, means that many eating places inevitably aim at pleasing travellers who want to break their journey without going too far from the main roads and who are not particularly interested in the local specialities, apart from the wine.

Because Champagne is, in many parts, flattish, and because it has no true natural boundaries, some gastronomic writers have found it dull as regards cuisine. Others have dismissed it as a region in which the wines won't go with the foods. This seems both inaccurate and ignorant. But it is certainly strongly influenced by neighbouring areas: what about the game and pâtés of the Ardennes and the Franco-Belgian border to the north; the vegetables, cheeses and dairy products of the Île de France and Paris; the sausages, quiches and hearty fare such as *choucroute* from Alsace and Lorraine to the east, and the fine fish and meat stews from Burgundy to the south? All these may be found.

Meat and Fish Dishes

Champagne has, felicitously, been described as a 'blonde countryside' because of its wheat, its sheep and Brie cheese (although this, strictly, is of Île de France origin). To this blondness may be added the pig and all the products of this often pale-skinned, light-fleshed animal. The Sainte Ménéhould area of the Marne, near Lorraine, is renowned for all types of pork products. Trotters, poached and grilled, feature on menus as *pieds de porc à la Ste. Ménéhould* and are perhaps the most famous, but there are numerous other pork dishes. The wild boar is still hunted up in the Ardennes; I remember one hotel where the owners actually kept a family of them in an enclosure in the garden for special gastronomic occasions. Boar (*sanglier*) is definitely game, but it is the *marcassin* (a youngster of less than six months) or the *bête rousse* (up to a year old) that will feature on menus. The pig also produces the smoked ham of the Ardennes, and is the base for the well-known pâtés made in that region. It is also responsible for the ham (*jambon*) that is a Reims speciality, and the *jambonneau*, which is a small-scale ham or hock; recipes often enclose the hams in a pastry case, and pigeons and small game birds are also often served *en croûte* (in a crust) in this way.

Then there are the many examples of the sausage family: *boudins* are excellent country fare (either as *boudin noir*, akin to the British black pudding, or as the milder *boudin blanc*, which is usually made with chicken). The *boudin Ste. Ménéhould* is traditionally made with rabbit (*lapin*), a humble form of game that is used in many pâtés or *civets* (stews). So is hare, which often appears in *civet de lièvre* (what we should term "jugged hare").

The most famous regional sausage, however, is the *andouille* and its relation, the *andouillette*; the former is essentially a tripe sausage, usually based on pork, but it can be made with other meat or game and is sometimes a smoked sausage – you will find examples in a *charcuterie* (delicatessen) if you are shopping for a picnic.

Andouillettes are supposed to have first been made by the pork butchers of Arras, outside the Champagne region; the Arras version became famous and sought-after, so the makers coloured the outside of the sausage (usually fatter than the ordinary British type) red, getting themselves the nickname of "Redguts". *Andouillettes* are now found in many parts of northern France. They are rather rich, but pleasantly succulent, and anyone who enjoys chitterlings should try this luxury version. *Andouillettes de mouton* (mutton) are a speciality of Troyes and famous as the sausage that saved that town: in the wars of religion in the sixteenth century the troops besieging Troyes actually breached the walls, but they then immediately stopped to gorge themselves on the *andouillettes* from the local shops and stalls, so that the inhabitants were able to muster their forces and drive out the invaders.

There are also types of sausages made from fish – *cervelat* (saveloy) *de poissons*, and also *cervelat de brochet* (pike) which includes potatoes. The supreme pike sausage, however, is the *quenelle*, which is found in many northern regions. It is usually sausage-shaped, but I have known it round, so that it may best be described as an apotheosis of a fishball, very light indeed and usually served with a somewhat rich sauce after being poached. The pike, with its underslung Habsburg-like jaw, is found in many rivers in northern France, but it is a rather dull, coarse fish if cooked in ordinary ways, whereas when pounded and formed into *quenelles* it is a luxury dish.

Quenelles can be made of poultry or some types of game too. *Pain à la reine* is a type of fish mousse, usually including pike. The queen referred to may be Maria Leczinska, wife of Louis XV and daughter of the exiled King Stanislas of Poland, whose elegant court at Nancy – not far away – evolved several excellent recipes that have survived to this day.

Small birds are used to make a variety of dishes, including pâtés made from thrushes (*grives*) and quails (*cailles*), and they are sometimes roasted and served in vine leaves. It should be remembered that, in many wine regions, the small birds feed on the grapes and become succulent as a result.

River fish include *carpe* (carp), *truite* (trout), *anguille* (eel) and *barbillon* (barbel), which may be used to make a *pochouse*, a type of stew of fish in white wine. This is also a Burgundy dish, but, made with Champagne, it is inevitably different. Up on the Belgian frontier there are *écrevisses* (crayfish) in some rivers, and some restaurants make a speciality of the *matelote*, another type of fish stew, which can be made with either white or red wine. There are also local snails (*escargots*), which of course will be served with garlic butter.

A type of egg and cheese pastry, called a *gougère*, is a speciality of the Aube. The *potée champenoise* is a typical substantial soup which contains meat (usually pork), possibly chicken, sausages and/or chunks of ham, plus vegetables and potatoes – a meal in itself.

Choucroute (pickled cabbage) is another dish that Champagne has taken from Alsace Lorraine: it can, in a luxury version, include several sorts of meat (as ever, certain pig products) and game, vegetables and sausages. However, if it is described as *"royale"* or *"à la Champagne"*, it arrives in its mounded form at table, with a small bottle of Champagne on top – this, poured over the whole, certainly conveys an impression of luxury, but I don't know that it makes very much difference to the flavour of this robust and piquant dish.

An excellent regional salad is made with dandelion leaves (*pissenlits*), which have a very fresh, almost bitter flavour; they are cooked in pork fat with vinegar, served with diced bacon (*lardons*) and sometimes potatoes, with the bacon fat poured over the greenery. (The dandelion leaves do not, to the best of my knowledge, have the effect on the consumer that their name implies.)

Sweets and Confectionary

There is a wide range of sweet dishes and confectionary, some probably originating in the convents of the great religious houses prior to the French Revolution. The finger-sized *biscuits de Reims* are the traditional accompaniment to a glass of Champagne, and it is permitted to dunk them in the wine; *massepain* (marzipan) and *pain d'épices* (a type of honeycake) are other Reims specialities. Macaroons are made throughout the region, and any *pâtissier* or *chocolatier* will have other prettily presented sweets vaunted as local delicacies. Such shops may also sell chocolates filled with marc or ratafia (see pages 37 to 39), and the *épicerie* (grocer) may have mustards, both in the form of sweets and real mustards, the latter often being made or packed in containers like the mushroom-shaped corks of Champagne.

Champagne is also a good region for fruit, when in season. Walnuts come from St. Gilles and, in the Ardennes, there is an apple called the *croquet des Ardennes*. There is also a famous pear, the Rousselet, which I have never discovered; it used to be a prized present for any visiting celebrity and for the kings of France after their coronation at Reims. The richness and juiciness of this *"poire tapée"* (the adjective means overflowing or abundant) is said to be such that it is simply not possible to market the fruit, as it is too delicate. If you can track the Rousselet down, it would obviously be a special treat.

Cheeses

Many of the cheeses that the traveller in Champagne will be offered have their origins outside the region itself, but certain of them are worth mentioning because of their affinity to the wines. There are, however, some specifically local cheeses as well.

Barberey is sometimes also known as "*Fromage de Troyes*", or "*Troyes Cendré*". It is made from cows' milk and is flat and round, with a greyish outside – hence the *cendré* (ashy) part of the name. It is slightly creamy in texture. There are several other versions of this sort of cheese, including the one called *Les Riceys*, made in the region. *Boursault* is a good creamy cheese produced in the region by a Monsieur Boursault after World War II.

Langres is a good cow milk cheese, very white in colour and slightly friable, moderately fat in style. It is vaguely triangular in shape, with a flat top. The best come from Poiseul, also from the Bassigny region. This cheese has a strong smell but it is not particularly fierce on the palate, although it possesses a definite character.

Chaource is a fine cow milk cheese, usually being round, cone-shaped and rather thick in format. It has a fattish style and gets its name from a type of Langres cheese, but it comes from Neuilly-sur-Suize. The outside is reddish-brown or tawny. It is agreeably rich in texture with a pleasant, milky smell.

Ervy or *Ervy-le-Châtel* is a cow milk cheese, cone-shaped and white in colour. It is mild in flavour although some find it smells vaguely of mushrooms. It comes principally from Ervy in the Aube.

Coulommiers is also made from cows' milk, principally in the Île de France but also in Champagne. It is a flattish, moderately-sized rounded cheese. The outside is pale in colour, with reddish-orange streaks; the smell is fairly strong, but intense and refined, and the flavour is somewhat related to Brie – in fact it is in some ways a small-scale version of this cheese. Although *Coulommiers* was originally a farmhouse cheese, it is increasingly being made in dairies. *Fromage à la pie* is a fresh version of *Coulommiers*, and the seldom-encountered *Macquelines* is another type, perhaps somewhat stronger in flavour.

The *Baguette-Laonnaise* is made in both the Île de France and Champagne, from cows' milk. It is usually oblong in form, with a brownish colour outside, a very pronounced smell – something akin to Camembert – and definite, strong taste.

Boulette de Cambrai is a farmhouse cheese, made around Cambrai and so outside the Champagne region, but it sometimes found on cheeseboards there. It is a round, ball-like cheese, very white in colour, with a light, fresh taste.

Brie is, strictly, an Île de France cheese nowadays, but at one time it was included in the former County of Champagne. So, as it is almost certain to feature in Champagne restaurants, it is included here. The 'Province de la Brie' is east of Paris, along the lower part of the Marne Valley, and the cheese is one of the greats of the world.

Brie is made from cows' milk and, in format, is a thin, largish round, varying in diameter according to type: the two main sizes are the big *grand moule* and the smaller *petit moule*. The outside is pure white, the inner cheese somewhat paler; the knowing usually test the cheese to see that it 'gives' slightly to the pressure of a finger, as it is hard and slightly chalky in texture when unripe. At its peak, a fine *Brie* has an intense, lingering smell – a true bouquet; the flavour is also very definite, marked but not aggressively strong. When eaten it should be soft and at the stage of becoming runny so that, when serving a whole cheese, small props have to be placed alongside the cut edges to prevent the cheese oozing from its skin. It is cut in long wedges and, if the cheeseboard holds a large wedge, then this too should be cut in a cake-like slice, along the length of the wedge: it is unfair and greedy to cut the tip off a *Brie* that is '*à point*' – that is, absolutely ripe – which it can be, if properly kept, within a matter of hours after previously being quite firm.

Brie has been made probably since the eighth century and Charlemagne is said to have liked it. In 1217, Blanche of Navarre, Countess of Champagne, sent 200 cheeses to King Philip Augustus of France. *Brie* was also used as a present by the poet, Charles d'Orléans, to his friends, and Henri IV said it was the best cheese he knew of. In Rabelais' *Gargantua et Pantagruel*, Gargantua sent *Brie* to his parents. Poets wrote in its praise, and in the sixteenth century the itinerant merchants of Paris cried its virtues in the streets. 'Le Grand Condé' (Louis II) celebrated his victory of Rocroi (1643) with *Brie* and red wine; Queen Maria Leczinska made *bouchées à la reine* (cheese puffs) with *Brie*; and the wretched Louis XVI, on the royal family's flight to Varennes at the time of the French Revolution, actually asked for *Brie* (and, it is said, the region's famous trotters) when he was captured. One contemporary writer then noted that, as *Brie* was loved by nobility and peasant alike, it "preached the doctrine of equality long before this was widely known".

At the Congress of Vienna, in 1815, *Brie* got its tag of "King of cheeses, cheese of kings". This Congress, of which it was said that "It dances but doesn't do anything", was much occupied with the pleasant adjuncts to civilised life, and the delegates are reported to have argued about the relative virtues of their various national cheeses. I don't, myself, believe in the assertion of a French gastronomic guide that the Duke of Wellington "entered Chester", as this is a cheese non-existent in Britain (although somewhat similar to Cheshire or an orange Cheddar when found in France), but it is possible that Metternich, definitely a lover of food and drink, did vaunt the cheeses of Bohemia. However, Talleyrand, of whom it was somewhat pertinently said that *Brie* was the only monarch to whom he had always been faithful, carried away the honours with the French cheese. There are various types of *Brie*, but the *Brie de Meaux, fermier* (farmhouse made), is supposed to be the best. Other types include the *Brie du Coulommiers* or *Brie petit moule* (the smaller rounded type), *Brie laitier*, made from pasteurised milk and often sold in segments in wedge-shaped boxes, *Brie de Melun*, which is available in various types, sometimes as a fresh cheese, and *Brie de Montereau*. One reference book states that a *Brie de Meaux* has a slightly nutty flavour, the *Brie de Coulommiers* is smoother and lighter, and the *Brie de Melun* is more full-bodied in taste.

APPENDIX 1

Sparkling Wines that are not Champagne

The only *appellation contrôlée* wine of France that does not need to state its A.C. on its label is Champagne: the name stands alone and suffices. The word "Champagne" cannot be used in the E.E.C. countries to mean anything except the sparkling wine of the Champagne vineyard. Even if the Champagne method is followed in detail to produce another fine sparkling wine, the description *"Méthode Champenoise"* is merely a description; the wine itself must bear its own *appellation d'origine contrôlée*.

There are many first-rate sparkling wines made in this way, including Blanquette de Limoux and those of Saumur (where the firm of Ackermann Laurence was founded by the son of a Champenois who, convalescing in the Loire, fell in love with the daughter of a local banker. The fathers set up the young people in business.) There is also Vouvray, where the sparkling wine makers are proud of the fact that it was the vignerons of Vouvray who, after the *phylloxera* ravages in the nineteenth century (see page 15) went up to assist in the rehabilitation of the Champagne vineyards. Seyssel makes a Champagne method sparkler, as does Alsace – one of the great nineteenth century wine makers was a friend of the head of a Reims establishment.

The "Spanish Champagne" case took place in London between the Costa Brava Wine Company, who had been selling a sparkling wine, Perelada, made by the Champagne method in Spain and, at the final hearing in 1960, twelve Champagne houses. Litigation had been going on for two years before but, at what some French newspapers termed "The Second Battle of the Marne", it was decided that in Britain the Spanish company could not label or sell their wine under any name that included the word "Champagne". In France, of course, they would not be allowed to do so either.

However, an agreement was signed in 1973 between France and Spain that tightens up the control of the use of the word "Champagne".

According to this, the use of the word "Champagne" or its translated form (*Champaña* in Spanish) is forbidden for any wine not made in Champagne and not corresponding to the French Champagne regulations. This decree, made in June 1973, seems quite definite, but I have not noted its enforcement among the producers of Spanish sparkling wine made according to the Champagne method; presumably it will be easier to establish the sole right to the word "Champagne" if Spain becomes a member of the European Community. However the C.I.V.C., zealous in its protective role, has rightly brought my attention to the existence of a decree that I think has been insufficiently publicised. Certainly, if you want a Champagne-method sparkling wine in Spain – where some first-rate ones are made – it will invariably be referred to as *"Champaña"* and not simply as *"Espumoso"* (sparkling).

There is no restraint on the Russians' use of *"Champanski"*, nor on references to "Champagne" with wines that are made in the Champagne way – and even those that are not, but which are sparkling – that come from various other countries outside the scope of legislation established in France and the E.E.C. This is where the drinker needs to have a good look at the label, to make certain as to the method whereby the wine in the bottle has been made sparkling.

In the U.S.A., for example, wines legally sold with the word "Champagne" on their labels and the place of their origin, may have the phrase "fermented in bottle" added to the description: this means – to abridge a complex procedure – that the wine will have been fermented in bottle, but that it will have been decanted (under pressure) and rebottled before being offered for sale. This is known as the 'transfer method'. It is used for many sparkling wines made in a number of countries, including some made in Germany, where huge quantities of *Sekt* (as their sparkling wine is often called) are consumed. But in the U.S.A. the term "fermented in *this* bottle" will mean that the wine has in fact spent all its life in the same one bottle – in other words, that the Champagne method has been followed.

This transfer method, a version of which is used to make most of the Asti spumante now produced, is halfway between the Champagne method and that termed *"méthode Charmat"* (after its perfector), or *"cuve close"* (sealed vat). Again, in very simple terms, this means that the wine is handled in a large vat instead of a bottle, the vat being sealed so that the carbon dioxide gas cannot escape. Monsieur Charmat's best-known wine is Veuve du Vernay.

Finally, wines can be made fizzy by simply pumping carbon dioxide into them. It used to be said that one could generally tell these by the large bubbles, coarse flavour and the fact that they went flat very quickly, but nowadays improved techniques have enabled makers to produce wines in this way that are not to be scorned. Among these 'gasified' wines are many that are only slightly sparkling or *pétillant*, and they are increasingly made all over the world, as it is found that drinkers in hot countries appreciate the slight tingle of the mini-fizz; in addition, the judicious use of carbon dioxide has been found both to preserve the freshness of what might otherwise be a short-lived white wine and to prevent its oxidising or turning a dark, dreary colour.

In case of confusion, it is worth stressing that the term *mousseux* means a wine that is fully sparkling. Champagne, of course, is fully sparkling (unless it is a *crémant* wine, see page 44) and therefore it could, very loosely, be referred to as a *vin mousseux*. But no scrupulous *sommelier* or informed wine lover would use this description when they might simply call it "Champagne", unless they were particularising, in which case they would say that a Champagne is "fully *mousseux*" to differentiate it from one that is only *crémant*. With other fully sparkling wines, the generic description is *mousseux*, with divisions as to the categories *méthode Charmat* or *produit en cuve close*, unless the prouder term *méthode Champenoise* can accurately be used.

As this book goes to press, E.E.C. regulations define certain details about sparkling wines within the Community (not to be confused with the regulations that apply in France). A wine that has more than one atmosphere of pressure and not more than two atmospheres behind its cork may be described as '*pétillant*'. If it has more than three atmospheres, then it is 'sparkling'. It is up to the producers of wines low in atmospheric pressure to decide whether the bottles should have an ordinary cork, a cork with a clip (like an *agrafe*), a screw-top or a mushroom cork that is wired down. In the U.K., however, any bottle sealed with a mushroom cork and 'dressed' so as to look as if it contains a sparkling wine will be obliged to pay full sparkling wine duty, just as if it were Champagne.

APPENDIX 2

The Champagne Wine Fraternity— Les Coteaux de Champagne

The wine fraternities of France are numerous and primarily organised so as to publicise the wines of their respective regions both in France and throughout the world. Some of them certainly had their origins in former times and might be then compared to the guilds or mercantile companies of the Middle Ages.

The Champagne fraternity or wine order, however, had an aristocratic beginning. The poet and critic, Nicolas Boileau (1636 – 1711), respected for his shrewd judgments on contemporary writers, described the origins of *"les Coteaux"* in a posthumous work that appeared in 1716. He related that the nickname was bestowed on "three notable noblemen, each particularly esteemed for his wines produced on the slopes adjacent to Reims. Each had his particular following . . . These lords, called *'les Coteaux'*, were the Commandeur de Souvré, the Duc de Mortemart and the Marquis de Sillery" (see also page 10).

The *Ordre des Coteaux de Champagne* as it exists today was established in 1956, with a *'Conseil chapitral'* of officers who, on occasions of ceremony, wear a purple-red robe and medieval flat cap of the same colour trimmed with white, and a broad ribbon of pink, cream and green, from which hangs the insignia of the order. This varies according to rank, but the main design shows the *pomponne*, a tall, tapering glass with a bulbous knob at the base instead of a foot, so that the glass cannot be set down but must be emptied at a draught. This *pomponne* is associated with Madame de Pompadour: tradition has it that this was the type of glass that was handed to the Marquise in her coach as refreshment when she passed through the region.

Thousands of men and women throughout the world have been made members of the *Ordre des Coteaux* at inauguration ceremonies, frequently held in spring and at vintage time, when the cry *"Haut le pomponne!"* means that everyone must raise his glass and then empty its contents in honour of the wine of Champagne.

APPENDIX 3

Champagne Festivals

The most important dates, as far as public celebrations are concerned, are January 22nd (the Feast of Saint Vincent, patron of wine growers), and the individual *'Cochelet'* rejoicings at the end of the vintage.

Generally, if January 22nd does not fall on a Saturday, villages will celebrate Saint Vincent on the nearest Saturday to that date. On the following Sunday there will often be a solemn mass, with the new wine carried in a preliminary procession through the streets to receive a formal blessing. At Épernay the occasion is one when the sales and exports of Champagne for the previous year are officially announced.

In midsummer (June 24th, Feast of Saint John the Baptist) there are also many celebrations, which again take place on the Saturday nearest the date. This is, of course, the summer solstice, and spectacles take place at Reims and Épernay and in many other villages, notably Cumières.

Various wine fairs are also organised, and for information about these the tourist should apply to the local Syndicat d'Initiative or information office, which is usually well signposted in French towns.

APPENDIX 4

Champagne and the Launching of Ships

It is unknown when the custom of breaking a bottle of Champagne over the bow of a ship about to be launched was begun, but it is now a firm tradition. It is also a tradition that it is a woman who names the ship and flings the bottle at the vessel as it begins to glide into the water. But there have been some curious incidents before the launching routine was perfected.

Some time ago a princess was performing the launching ceremony of a ship at Plymouth, in days when the bottle was not secured to anything but was simply thrown at the bows; the lady missed the ship but the bottle hit a spectator on the head, so hard that he later claimed – and received—substantial damages. Since that time the bottle has been tied on to the ship by a ribbon. But the thickness of Champagne bottles has also presented problems. Once, a ship about to be launched on Clydeside began to slide away from the V.I.P.'s platform before the woman launching it could hurl the bottle at its side, so she flung it after the ship as hard as she could. However, it bounced off the ship and swung back, then to be caught by the dockyard manager who threw it again – and missed. The christening party had therefore to leap into a launch and pursue the ship, so as to break the bottle at the third attempt. This is why, nowadays, the bottom of the dressed-up launching bottle is usually weighted with lead, so that it will definitely break at the first impact.

Then there was the episode when a Japanese Minister of Marine was launching a ship and the bottle swung short of the side, hanging there by its ribbon. But as soon as the ship entered the water, a sampan rushed up alongside, cut the ribbon and went off with the Champagne!

Some shipowners who have been total abstainers have attempted to use a non-alcoholic christening fluid for launching a ship, but this is generally regarded as a sign that bad luck will dog the vessel. Indeed, in 1853 a huge four-master, the *Great Republic*, then the biggest ship in the world, was christened with Cochituate water, which had been brought to Boston by the clipper builder, Donald McKay, for the occasion. This was at a time when the temperance movement was becoming very powerful in New England and, in publicising the use of a table water, McKay hoped to gain public favour. But what had really happened was that, during the night before the launching, some of the apprentices in the yard had got hold of the Champagne intended for the vessel's baptism, and drunk it all. McKay didn't replace it – and, as it so happened, the *Great Republic* caught fire soon after while loading; being made of oak and pine, she burnt furiously, the fire spreading to two other clippers nearby on the quay. For many years, it was told how McKay's meanness in not buying another bottle of Champagne had brought him almost to ruin.

Glossary of Wine Terms

The following vocabularies give certain terms that may be either difficult to find in a dictionary or, if they are given, may bear a different significance from that which they carry in relation to wine. Terms may vary from wine region to wine region and even a Frenchman would discover certain words peculiar to Champagne.

The vocabularies are divided into sections, according to the context in which the various words and phrases will most frequently occur. Naturally, anyone whose French is good will be able to assimilate and use them quite quickly. But someone whose French is somewhat hesitant may find that an English-speaking guide will use local words that can be difficult to translate quickly. If any conversation includes such words or similarly unfamiliar phrases, then the visitor may lose the thread of the whole conversation. So, for convenient reference, the aspects of the subject are sub-divided.

It is quite easy, for anyone in sympathy with a subject, to understand what is being said even in a language that the hearer cannot actually speak; the use of certain key words and phrases, in trade or technical conversations, is obvious. One can ask a question in English and get the answer back in French, with both parties to the conversation following the tenor of what is being discussed.

There is also the problem of certain expressions being easy to understand, but virtually impossible to translate. For example, '*un vin fin*' is not at all the same thing as 'a fine wine', any more than '*un grand vin*' is the same as 'a great wine'. (I would translate '*un vin fin*' as 'a wine of breed and distinction', and '*un grand vin*' as 'a wine of stature – memorable'.) In instances such as these the 'understanding of the heart' must come in; shades of meaning and association implied by even one word in a particular language may need a whole phrase to interpret them adequately into another. But here I have tried to keep the words and phrases within the meanings they might carry when being used in Champagne – as I would use them talking with friends. In other parts of France they might carry slightly different meanings.

People

Un caviste A cellar worker, but one definitely skilled in the care of the wine, of far greater standing than a mere 'hand'.

Le chef de cave The man responsible for making the wine, composing the cuvée and supervising the care of the wine throughout its stay in the cellar. He may actually be the head of the firm, and he is invariably an important and prized member of the establishment.

Un colporteur The man who, out in the vineyard, loads the filled baskets onto the lorries that will take the grapes to the press.

Un hordon The team of pickers, who work methodically across the vineyard.

Un négociant A shipper. In Champagne, the term is rather more precise, meaning the individual or the firm who actually makes the wine – as in *un négociant en vin de Champagne*. The term *un négociant-manipulant* is used either for the person or for the firm who both make and market the Champagne (see page 41). *Un récoltant-manipulant* is someone primarily concerned with care of the vines and growing the grapes, but who also actually makes Champagne.

Un oenologue A specialist in wine, highly qualified and often a chemist. He may be the same as *le chef de cave*.

Le patron Literally 'the boss' – the head of a concern.

Un porteur The person who, at vintage time, as a member of a picking team, is specially responsible for taking away the baskets of grapes as these are filled.

Un remueur The highly skilled cellar worker who shakes and turns the bottles so as to get the deposit in the wine down on to the first cork (see page 30).

Un vendangeur A vintager – one who picks the grapes.

Vines

Le cépage The variety of vine, hence often used to signify the type of grape, e.g. *Quel cépage?* – What grape (is it made from)?

Le débourrement The breaking out of the buds in early spring.

La fleuraison The flowering (of the vine) in early summer.

Le gel Frost.

La grappe The entire bunch of grapes.

Greffer To graft. *La porte greffe* is the disease-resistant stock onto which the vine destined to produce grapes is grafted.

La grêle Hail.

La pourriture Rot.

Le raisin The (single) individual grape.

La racine pivotante The taproot.

La sortie du raisin, or *La montre* The emergence of the minute bunches that will later become grapes.

La souche The vinestock or, as might be said colloquially, 'the foot' – i.e. the vine as it stands in the earth. To buy *sur souche* is to buy ahead of the vintage, or 'on spec'.

Tailler To prune (usually done in March).

La tige The stalk.

Les vendanges The vintage – the picking of the grapes.

Vintage time

La clayette The basketwork tray, usually propped on two *mannequins* (see below) on which the process of *épluchage* is carried out (see below).

Les épinettes The special cutters used by the vintagers for detaching clusters of grapes from the vines.

Épluchage The procedure of sorting through bunches of grapes out in the vineyard, so as to reject any that are inferior, either bunch by bunch or, more rarely, grape by grape (see page 23).

Le mannequin The large oval basket, traditionally used for transporting grapes from the vineyard to the press.

L'ouverture des vendanges The official date announced by the C.I.V.C. when picking of the grapes may be started.

Un vendangeoir The building that houses the pickers at vintage time, out in the vineyards. Sometimes it includes a presshouse and wine-making equipment as well.

Un vendangeur A vintager.

Soils and countryside

L'argile Clay.

Le calcaire Limestone.

La craie Chalk. *Une crayère* is a chalk pit and refers to the ancient excavations beneath many of the establishments (see page 5).

Les cendres noires Type of lignite deposit, found especially on the

Montagne de Reims and contributing so much to the soil that it is sometimes referred to as 'the black gold of Champagne'.

La Champagne The Champagne region.

La Champagne viticole The Champagne area that is under vines.

Un cru Literally 'a growth', but frequently used in wine areas to signify a specific vineyard and also sometimes a wine made from a single site. For the significance of *grand cru* see page 52.

Les Falaises Literally 'the cliffs', but in this context the hills of the Champagne region that are rich in a special type of chalk.

Un finage An individual growth, site or plot.

Le sable Sand. But *sabler* means to swig, knock back, swill – i.e. *sabler le Champagne* – to swill Champagne.

Le sous-sol The subsoil.

Le terroir The (type of) soil. *Le terrain* is simply 'the ground'.

Making the wine

L'agrafe The clip that fastens the first cork into the Champagne bottle.

Le bouchon The cork. *Le bouchage* is the process of corking, but in this context it usually means the second corking, when *le bouchon d'expédition*, or second cork, is inserted (see page 32).

Un bouchon couronne A crown cork (see page 29).

Le cellier The cellar. But, in this context, it generally means the above-ground wine store where the first part of the fermentation takes place.

Le cave The cellar (below ground) in a Champagne house. The use of this term, rather than that of *le cellier*, implies size and the premises being used for business. But it is quite usual for an ordinary person to refer to *"mon cave"* or even *"mes caves"*, signifying stocks or reserves of wine, not specifically the place where they are kept e.g. *J'ai toujours dix ou douze bouteilles de Champagne dans mon cave au garage* – I've always got ten or twelve bottles of Champagne in my cellar in the garage.

Coller To fine (see page 28).

Couper To blend. But, in this context, one would say *faire la cuvée*. The significance of *couper* tends to be somewhat slighting and implies an addition or to cut a wine with something else e.g. *Autrefois, les vins de Bordeaux étaient souvent coupés avec les vins du sud* – In former times, Bordeaux wines were often 'cut' with southern wines.

Une cuvée Here signifying a blend. *Une cuve* is a vat and, hence, *la cuvée* is the contents – i.e. a vatting. *Faire la cuvée* is to make up the blend of Champagne by combining the different wines in the vat. *Le vin de cuvée* is the first 2,000 litres of juice to flow from the press.

Débourbage The process whereby the must is cleaned and any obvious debris and impurities are removed – usually effected by a process of refrigeration or by the use of SO_2 (sulphur dioxide – the multi-purpose wine disinfectant).

Dégorger To disgorge (see page 32). *Le dégorgement* is the process whereby the first cork is removed and the second inserted. *Dégorgement à la volée* is the process of disgorging by hand, when the cork will fly out; *dégorgement à la glace* is disgorging when the neck of the bottle has been frozen, so that the pressure inside forces out the first cork with a pellet of ice holding the deposit.

Le dosage The sweetening added to the wine at the time of the insertion of the second cork (see page 33).

Fermenter To ferment.

Les lattes The lathes, which separate and support the rows of bottles laid on their sides to mature. During this period they are *sur lattes*.

La levure The yeast.

Le liqueur de tirage The booster of still Champagne and sugar added to the vat prior to the bottling of the wine (see page 28).

Le liqueur d'expédition The dosage (see page 33) of sugar and wine added when the second cork goes in to regulate the required sweetening.

La maie The special type of Champagne press (see page 25).

Un marc The 4,000 kg of grapes that are the contents of a *maie*.

La mise en masse The stacking of the bottles upside down *sur les pointes*.

Le moût The must – unfermented grape juice prior to its conversion into wine by the action of the yeasts.

Osciller To shake (the bottles – see page 30).

Peser To weigh – the grapes are weighed on their arrival at the presshouse.

Une presse A press. Not to be confused with the specialised Champagne press, the *maie*. *Une presse horizontale* can signify the type of press that contains a bag, operated so as to squeeze the grapes, or else a rotating press containing chains that strip off the grapes from the stalks. *Le pressurage* is the process of pressing.

La prise de mousse Literally, the adoption of the sparkle, the period when the bottled wines develop their vivacity in the spring after their vintage.

Pupitre The literal translation is 'a desk', but in Champagne it is a slotted board, set upright at the same sort of angle as an easel, in which the bottles are fitted for the process of *remuage*.

Remplissage The process of topping up.

Remueur The action of both shaking and rotating the bottles of Champagne. The process is *remuage*, the person who does it is a *remueur*.

Soutirer To rack.

Une serre A pressing. *Serrer* – to squeeze.

Sur les pointes When the bottles are stacked upside down, on their corks (see page 32).

Le vin de taille The 666 litres of juice that come from the press after the *vin de cuvée* (see page 26).

The bottle

Une bague carré – '*une bague*' usually means a ring; in this context it signifies the ledge or flange just below the lip of the bottle. The adjective *carré* means squared-off, and the type of bottle that has this sort of ledge is one made to take the *agrafe*, which grips it. *Une bague couronne* is a rounded-off ledge – such as will hold a crown cork (*un bouchon couronne*).

Le bouchon The cork; *le bouchon d'expédition* is the second cork – i.e. the cork which is inserted when the bottle goes away to be sold.

La capsule The capsule, or covering of the cork that extends down the neck of the bottle.

L'étiquette The label. *L'étiquette du collier* is the neck label. *La contre étiquette* is the back label.

Le muselet (de fil de fer) The muzzle (of wire) which secures the second cork in the bottle, the process being *ficelage*.

La plaque The metal cap that prevents the wire muzzle biting into the second cork.

Wines and tasting

Bien equilibré Well balanced.

Blanc de blancs White wine made from white grapes (see page 44).

Blanc de noirs White wine made from black grapes (see page 44).

Bouqueté Fragrant.

Corsé Full-bodied.

Cracher To spit. *Un crachoir* is a spittoon.

Crémant Not quite as sparkling as a wine that is fully *mousseux* (see page 44).

Déguster To taste (the verb that is always used for tasting wine). *Une dégustation* is a tasting.

Frais Cool, cold.

Frappé Iced.

Impeccable Impeccable – a useful word with which to compliment a great wine.

Mousseux Sparkling – signifying fully sparkling. *La mousse* is the sparkle.

La méthode Champenoise The Champagne process.

Net, nette Sound, flawless; term of high praise for a well-made wine.

Perlant Literally 'pearling', signifying wine with a very slight sparkle.

Pétillant Very slightly sparkling – something that can vary considerably.

Propre Clean – term of approbation for a well-made wine.

Récemment dégorgé Recently disgorged (see page 32).

Sans année Non-vintage. A vintage wine is one that is *millésimé* – i.e. dated.

Il se termine bien Literally 'it finishes well' (that is, it leaves the palate fresh, refreshed and probably wanting more).

Trinquer To clink (glasses).

Further Reading

Most good general books on wine have sections devoted to Champagne and the reader should be able to consult a number of these. Some note should be taken of the date of any book, however, because unfortunately a few overall guides to wine are very out-of-date, through no fault of the original authors, many of whom are now dead. The late André L. Simon wrote much about Champagne, as his early business career was devoted to selling Pommery in the United Kingdom; historically his work is very important, but he did not live to see many procedures that are now routine adopted by the producers.

The History of Champagne by André L. Simon (Ebury Press, 1962) is beautifully illustrated and, although now out of print, well worth consulting in libraries.

Champagne: The wine, the land and the people by Patrick Forbes (Gollancz, 1967) is the masterwork on the subject, always readable and superbly detailed. Mr. Forbes is now the head of Moët et Chandon (London) but, when researching for his book, he lived in Champagne and has an unparalleled experience of all the processes involved with the production of the wine.

Bollinger by Cyril Ray (Peter Davies, 1971) is an elegantly written account, not only of this great Champagne, but also of its setting. Mr. Ray is a journalist worthy of his subject, and his account of the social background to Champagne in general is essential reading.

Krug, House of Champagne by John Arlott (Davis-Poynter, 1976) is another well-written profile of an outstanding firm, with much concomitant information.

The Michelin maps for travellers are sheet Nos. 56 and 61, and the Michelin Green Guide *Nord de la France* includes the Champagne area. As regards overall guides, the individual must follow individual preference. There are many guides to specific towns and regions in French, and some of the great Champagne houses have commissioned individual histories of their establishments.

The Comité Interprofessionnel du Vin de Champagne in Épernay and Food from France (S.O.P.E.X.A., Nuffield House, 41 – 46 Piccadilly, London, W.1.) issue excellent promotional material and maps that those hoping to explore this underrated but subtly fascinating region should try to obtain. Kingsway Public Relations, 10 Doughty Street, London, W.C.1., who are the United Kingdom publicity officers for the C.I.V.C., likewise have plenty of leaflets and data available for serious enquirers.

Index

Ackermann, Laurence, 102
Alsace, 57, 102
Ambonnay, 36, 44, 65
Appellation d'Origine Contrôlée, 35, 51, 102
Arbanne vine, 19
Ardennes, 1, 57, 58, 96, 98
Arras, 96
Asti spumante, 103
Aube, 1, 16, 99
Avenay-Val-d'Or, 65
Avery, Ronald, 87–8
Avize, 67
Ay, 8, 9, 16, 21–2, 38, 44, 45, 65, 84
Ayala, 16, 42, 60

Bar-sur-Aube, 58, 69
Bassigny, 99
Bergères-lès-Vertus, 67
Besserat de Bellefon, 60
Bethon, 68, 69
Bissinger, 16
Black Velvet, 85, 92
Blanc de blancs, 21, 44, 71, 73, 78, 91
Blanc de noirs, 21–2, 44
Boileau, Nicolas, 105
Bollinger, 16, 60
Bordeaux, 90
Bottles, 10, 17, 46ff, 79–81
Bottling, 28ff, 46–7
Bouzy, 36, 45, 65
Bouzy-Barancourt, 45
Brandy, 38
Brut, 33–4
Bucks Fizz, 92–3
Burgundy, 19, 57, 87–8, 90
Butler, Frank Hedges, 15

Buyer's Own Brands (B.O.B.), 43, 91

Canard-Duchêne, 61
Carbon dioxide, 102–3
Casks, 10, 38, 48ff
Cellars, 59–63
Champagne: Cocktail, 93–4
  Colour, 44, 70ff
  Establishments, visiting, 57, 58, 59ff, 66, 69
  'Riots', 16
  Routes, 55, 58, 64ff
  Serving, 77ff
  Tours, 57, 58
Champillon, 66
Chardonnay vine, 19, 20, 21, 26, 36, 38, 68
Charlemagne, 100
Charles II, 10–11; V, 9; VII, 8, 9
Charleville-Mézières, 57
Charmat, M., 103
Châtillon-sur-Marne, 66
Chigny-les-Roses, 64
Churchill, Sir Winston, 47
Clairvaux, 69
Climate, 3–4, 19, 65
Clicquot, 14, 73
  Madame, 13
  -Ponsardin, 12, 41, 47
  Veuve, 42, 61, 89
Clovis, 7, 8
Cochelet, The, 25, 106
Collery, 45
Colombey-les-Deux-Églises, 57
Comité Interprofessionel du Vin de Champagne (C.I.V.C.), 18, 22, 35, 41, 52, 56, 103

INDEX

Compiègne, Forest of, 57
Confrérie Saint-Paul Saint-Vincent, 69
Cooperative Vinicole de Mancy, 61
Corks, 10, 17, 28–30, 32–3, 34, 35, 47, 52, 71, 72, 80–3
Costa Brava Wine Company, 102
Côte des Blancs, 1, 66, 67
Coteaux Champenois, 35, 36, 68, 87, 88–9, 90, 105
Cramant, 67
Crayères, 5–6, 12, 55, 58
Crémant, 28, 44–5, 88, 91, 102
Crown cork, 29–30, 48–50
Cumières, 36, 44, 66
Cuvée, 11, 26, 27, 73, 90, 91

Damery, 16, 66
De Castellane, 61
Delmotte, 15
De Luxe Champagnes, 45–6
Demi-sec, 34, 89
Deutz & Gelderman, 42
Disgourging, 32–3
Dizy, 16, 44, 66
Domitian, 7
Dosage, 33–4
Doux, 34

Edward III, 9
E.E.C., 103, 104
Épernay, 16, 55, 56, 58, 65, 66, 67, 68, 106
Épluchage, 23–4
Extra-dry, 34

'*Faux de Verzy*', 55, 65
Fermentation, 10, 27, 28
Festivals, 106
Fine, 38–9
Fining, 28
Food, 60, 67, 68, 87ff, 95ff
Forbes, Patrick, 5, 7, 8, 20, 25, 47
'French 75', 93

Gelderman, 16
Glasses, 71ff, 83–6
Goulet, George, 45, 61
Goyard, 38
Grand Cru, 52
Grandes Marques, 41–2
Grapes, 19–22, 38, 58
Grauves, 67
Growers, 40–1

Hamilton, Sir William and Lady, 13
Harben, Philip, 42–3, 89
Haute-Marne, 1
Hautvilliers, 11, 16, 66
Heidsieck, 12
   Charles, 42, 61
   Monopole, 42, 61
Henri IV, 9, 65, 66, 100
Henriot & Co., 61
Henry V, 57; VIII, 9

Île de France, 99, 100
Institut National des Appellations d'Origine, 41

Joan of Arc, 8, 9
Jouy-lès-Reims, 64

King Pimm's, 92
Krug, 42, 46, 62

Labels, 51–2
Lalique, René, 84
Lanson Père et Fils, 12, 42, 62, 73
Launching ships, 108–9
Le Mesnil-sur-Oger, 67
Le Nôtre, 65
Leo X, 9
Lepître, Abel, 60
Le Tellier, Michel, 65
Liqueur de tirage, 28
Louis XIV, 10; XV, 65; XVI, 10
Louvois, 65
Ludes-le-Coquet, 64

Mailly-Champagne, 64
Mansart, 65
Marc, 37–8
Mareuil-sur-Ay, 66
Marie Antoinette, 83
Marne, 1, 16, 17, 65, 66, 100
Martel, G.H., 62
Massé Père et Fils, 62
Merchants, 41, 50, 52
Mercier, 42, 56, 59, 62
Méthode Champenoise, 102, 104
Méthode Charmat, 103
Metternich, 101
Moët
   et Chandon, 12, 42, 47, 56, 62, 66, 67
   Jean-Rémy, 13
Montagne de Reims, 1, 17, 64

Mont Sinaï, 65
Mousse, 30, 44, 70ff, 81, 85, 87, 88, 104
Mumm, G.H., 62-3
Must, 25-6, 27

Napoleon, 13
Négociant-manipulant, 41, 52
Nelson, 13
Neuilly-sur-Suize, 99
Non-vintage Champagne, 42-3, 50, 71, 78

Ordre des Coteaux de Champagne, 10, 105
Orleans, Charles d', 100

Paradis, Michel, 69
Paris, 55, 57, 58, 95, 100
Pérignon, Dom Pierre, 11-12, 66
Perrier
  Family, 56
  Joseph, Fils & Co, 62
  -Jouët, 42, 63
  Laurent, 37
  Veuve-Laurent, 62
Pétillant, 44, 104
Petit Meslier vine, 19
Philip Augustus, 100
Philliponat, 63
Phylloxera vastatrix, 15, 102
Pinot vine, 19, 20, 38
  Meunier, 19, 20-1
  Noir, 14, 19, 20
Piper Heidsieck, 42, 59, 63
Pol Roger, 42, 46, 63
  Maurice, 16-17
Pommery, 14
  & Greno, 6, 42, 63, 73
Pompadour, Madame de, 12, 105
Ponsardin, M., 13
Premier Cru, 52
Pressing, 25-7
Pupitres, 30-1

Rabelais, 100
Ratafia, 36-7
Red wines, 19
Reims, 7, 9, 10, 13, 16, 17, 53, 55, 56, 58, 59, 64, 68, 84, 89, 102, 106
Religious Houses, 8, 11, 65, 69
Rémi, Saint, 7, 8, 55
Remuage, 30-2, 51
Resistance, 17-18
Revolution, French, 100

Rilly, 44
Roederer, 42, 43, 73, 89-90
  Louis, 62
  Madame, 47
Romans, 5-6, 7, 10
Rosé/Pink Champagne, 44, 45, 73, 78, 89-90
Rothschild, Baron Philippe de, 43
Ruinart, 6, 12, 42, 63
  Dom, 66

Saint-Evremond, Marquis de, 10
St. Lié, 64
Saintsbury, Professor George, 14
Saint Vincent, 106
Saran, 67
Saumur, 102
Sauvignon, 21
Sec, 34
Seyssel, 102
Sézanne, 7, 58, 67, 68
Shippers, 40, 50
Sillery, 13, 14, 64
  Marquis de, 10
Simon, André, 14
Single growth Champagnes, 45
Société des Producteurs, 63
Soil, 2, 19, 65
Soissons, 53, 64
Spanish sparkling wines, 31, 102ff
Still wines, 35-6

Taittinger, 42, 63
  Madame Claude, 83-4
Talleyrand, 101
Tasting, 25, 29, 68, 69, 70ff
Trouillard, 43
Troyes, 55, 56, 58, 97

Urban II, 8, 66

Vertus, 13, 67
Verzenay, 44, 64
Verzy, 64, 65
Villédommange, 44, 64
Vin gris, 9
Vintage, The, 22ff, 57
Vintages, 14, 17, 27-8, 43-4, 71, 89, 90
Vogüé, Comte Robert de, 18
Vouvray, 102

Wars, 3, 9, 13, 14, 16-18, 50, 55, 66
Wellington, Duke of, 13, 101